Broken relationships…fear…loneliness…
habitual sin…guilt…spiritual dryness….
These are just a few of many causes of dis-
couragement. In the pages that follow, David
Wilkerson shows you that these problems
are no reason to give up. He maintains that
hope is always present because God is on
our side. Through scriptural promises and
enlightening illustrations, he provides reassurance that God will help you through your
struggles. His message is filled with comfort
and reassurance that God will never abandon you. You can claim victory over discour-
agement and be healed of your heartaches
because God has a plan and purpose for
your life.

Have You Felt Like Giving Up Lately?

David Wilkerson

Fleming H. Revell
A Division of Baker Book House Co
Grand Rapids, Michigan 49516

Scripture quotations are from the King James Version of the Bible.

Library of Congress Cataloging-in-Publication Data

Wilkerson, David R.
  Have you felt like giving up lately?

  1. Christian life—1960-   I. Title.
BV4501.2.W5198   248.4   80-10402
ISBN 0-8007-8481-2

Twenty-fourth printing, December 1995

Printed in the United States of America

Contents

Foreword

This book has been in the making for years. It was born from a cry, deep in my heart, to help hurting people.

I travel, preaching crusades, across this great land; and I meet so many hurting people who can't seem to find relief from their problems. These hurting people are often divorced or separated. Some are lonely young people who can't find love. Others are caught in a web of despair, suffering from guilt, condemnation, depression, and fear.

It is my firm conviction that, in one way or another, we are all hurting. We all need healing of our inner hurts. We need to know how to get hold of a genuine peace and a true freedom from the bondage of besetting sins. It is sin that causes so many of our problems and hurts.

I hope this book will help multitudes of Christians find true healing. Already, a great number of friends have been healed as a result of the messages included here.

Healing is a process. Read every chapter and witness that powerful healing process take place in your life. I can say that with boldness, because I know these messages were born in prayer, bathed in tears, tested through personal sorrow and suffering, and, most important of all, founded on the true Word of God.

Have You Felt Like Giving Up Lately ?

1

When You Hurt

In one way or another, we are all hurting. Everyone is in the same boat. Even the laughing, happy-go-lucky crowd is hurting. They try to hide their hurt by drinking and joking, but it won't go away.

Who hurts? The parents of a prodigal son or daughter. Millions of parents have been deeply wounded by children who have rejected their counsel. Those loving parents grieve over the deception and delinquency of children who were once tender and good.

The victims of broken homes are hurting. The abandoned wife whose husband rejected her for another woman is hurting. The husband who lost the love of a wife is hurting. The children who lost their security are hurting.

Others suffer illness: cancer, heart problems, and a myriad of other human diseases. To be told by a doctor, "You have cancer; you may die!" has to be terrifying. Yet many reading this message have experienced such pain and agony.

Lovers break up. A boyfriend or girlfriend walks away, trampling on what was once a beautiful relationship. All that is left is a broken, wounded heart.

And what about the unemployed? The despondent ones whose dreams have collapsed? The shut-ins? The prisoners? The homosexuals? The alcoholics?

It is true! In one way or another we are all hurting. Every person on earth carries his own burden of pain and hurt.

There Is No Physical Cure

When you are deeply hurt, no person on this earth can shut out the innermost fears and deepest agonies. The best of friends cannot really understand the battle you are going through or the wounds inflicted on you.

Only God can shut out the waves of depression and feelings of loneliness and failure which come over you. Faith in God's love alone can salvage the hurt mind. The bruised and broken heart that suffers in silence can be healed only by a supernatural work of the Holy Spirit, and nothing short of divine intervention really works.

God has to step in and take over. He has to intercept our lives at the breaking point, stretch forth His loving arms, and bring that hurting body and mind under His protection and care. God must come forth as a caring Father and demonstrate that He is there, making things turn out for good. He must, by His own power, dispel the storm clouds, chase away the despair and gloom, wipe away the tears, and replace the sorrow with peace of mind.

Why Me, Lord?

What hurts most is that you know your love for God is strong, yet you can't seem to understand what He is trying to work out in your life. If you were cold toward His love, you could understand why prayers went unanswered. If you were running from God, you could probably understand why the testings and severe trials kept coming on. If you were a down-and-out sinner, who despised the things of God, you could bring yourself to believe you deserved to be hurt badly. But you are not running; you are not rejecting Him in any way. You long to do His perfect will. You yearn to please God and want only to serve Him with all that is in you. That is why your hurting is so debilitating. It makes you feel there is something terribly wrong with you. You question your spiritual depth, and at times, you even question your sanity. From somewhere deep inside you, a voice whispers, "Maybe I'm defective, somehow. Maybe I'm being hurt so deeply because God can't see much good in me. I must be so out of His will; He has to discipline me to make me obedient."

Friends Try So Hard to Help

A bruised or broken heart causes the most excruciating pain known to mankind. Most other human hurts are only physical, but a heart that is wounded must carry a pain that is both physical and spiritual. Friends and loved ones can help soothe the physical pain of a broken heart. When they are there, laughing, loving, and caring, the physical pain eases, and there is temporary relief. But night falls, and with it comes the terror of spiritual agony. Pain is always worse in the night. Loneliness falls like a cloud, when the sun disappears. The hurting explodes when you are all alone, trying to understand how to cope with the inner voices and fears that keep surfacing.

Your friends, who really don't understand what you are going through, offer all kinds of easy solutions. They get impatient with you. They are mostly happy and carefree, at the time; and they can't understand why you don't simply snap out of it. They suspect you are indulging in self-pity. They remind you the world is filled with heartbroken, hurting people who have survived. More often, they want to pray that one-time, cure-all, solve-everything prayer. You are told to "release your faith, claim a promise, confess a cure, and walk away from your despair."

That's all well and good, but it's preaching that usually comes from Christians who have never known much suffering in their own lives. They are like Job's baby-sitters, who knew all the answers but who could not relieve his pain. Job said to them, ". . . ye are all physicians of no value" (Job 13:4). Thank God for well-meaning friends, but if they could experience your agony for even one hour, they would be changing their tunes. Put them in your place just once, feeling what you feel, experiencing the inner pain you carry, and they would be saying to you, "How in the world can you take it? I couldn't handle what you are going through!"

Time Heals Nothing

Then there is that age-old cliché, "Time heals all wounds." You are told to hang in there, put on a smile, and wait for time to anesthetize your pain. But I suspect all the rules and clichés about loneliness are coined by happy, unhurt people. It sounds good, but it is not true. Time heals nothing; only God heals!

When you are hurting, time only magnifies the pain. Days and weeks go by, and the agony hangs on. The hurting won't go away, no matter what the calendar says. Time may push the pain deeper into the mind, but one tiny memory can bring it to the surface.

Truthfully, it doesn't help much, either, to know Christians have suffered before you down through the ages. You can identify with the suffering of Bible characters who survived tremendous ordeals of pain. But knowing that others have gone through great battles doesn't calm the hurt in your own bosom. When you read how they victoriously came out of their battles, and you still haven't, it only adds to your hurt. It makes you feel as though they were very close to God to receive such answers to their prayers. It makes you feel unworthy of the Lord, because your problem lingers on, in spite of all your spiritual efforts.

Double Trouble

People seldom get hurt just once. Most who hurt can show you other wounds also. Pain is layered over pain. A broken heart is usually a tender, fragile one. It is easily broken because it is not protected by a hard shell. Tenderness is mistaken for vulnerability, by the hard-shelled heart. Quietness is misjudged as a weakness. A total giving of oneself to another is mistaken as coming on too strong. The heart that is not afraid to admit its need of love is misjudged as being too sexually oriented.

It follows then that a tender heart which reaches for love and understanding is often the easiest to break. Hearts that are open and trusting are usually the ones that are wounded the most. This world is filled with men and women who have rejected the love offered to them from a heart that is gentle and tender. Those strong, hard-shelled hearts that trust no one, hearts that give so little, hearts that demand love be constantly proved, hearts that are always calculating, hearts that are always manipulating and self-serving, hearts that are afraid to risk are the ones that seldom get broken. They don't get wounded, because there is nothing to wound. They are too proud and self-centered to allow anyone else to make them suffer in any way. They go about breaking other hearts and trampling on the fragile souls who touch their lives, simply because they are so thick and dull at heart themselves, and they think everyone should be just as they are. The hard hearts don't like tears. They hate commitment. They feel smothered when asked to share from their own hearts.

Heartbreakers Do Not Get Off Easy

Part of the pain a broken heart must suffer is the thought that the offender, the heartbreaker, is going to get away with it all. The heart says, "I am the one hurt and wounded; yet I'm the one who pays the price. The offender gets off scot-free, when he should pay for what he did." That's the problem with crosses; the wrong person usually gets crucified. But God keeps the books, and on Judgment Day, the books will be balanced. But even in this life, heartbreakers and people wounders pay a high price. No matter how they try to justify their hurtful actions, they cannot drown out the cries of the ones they have wounded. Like the blood of Abel, which cried out from the ground, the cries of a broken heart can pierce the barrier of time and space and terrorize the hardest of hearts. Hurts are usually caused by outright lies, and every liar must eventually be brought to justice.

Is there a balm for a broken heart? Is there healing for those deep, inner hurts? Can the pieces be put back together and the heart be made even stronger? Can the person who has known such horrible pain and suffering rise out of the ashes of depression and find a new and more powerful way of life? Yes! Absolutely yes! And if not, then God's Word would be a hoax, and God Himself would be a liar. That cannot be!

Let me share a few simple thoughts about how to cope with your hurt.

Stop trying to figure out how and why you got hurt. What has happened to you is a very common ailment among mankind. Your situation is not unique at all. It is the way of human nature. Whether you were right or wrong means absolutely nothing at this point. All that matters now is your willingness to move on in God and trust His mysterious workings in your life. The Bible says:

> . . . think it not strange concerning the fiery trial which is to try you, as though some strange thing happened unto you: But rejoice, inasmuch as ye are partakers of Christ's sufferings; that, when his glory shall be revealed, yet may be glad also with exceeding joy.
>
> 1 Peter 4:12, 13

God didn't promise to give you a painless way of life: He promised you a way of escape. He promised you help to bear your pain and to give you strength to put you back on your feet when weakness makes you stagger.

Most likely you did what you had to do. You moved in the will of God, honestly following your heart. You went into it with an open heart, willing to give of yourself. Love was your motivation. You did not abort the will of God; someone else did. If that were not true, you would not be the one who is hurting so. You are hurt because you tried to be honest.

You can't understand why things blew up in your face, when God seemed to be leading all along. Your heart asks, "Why did God allow me to get into this in the first place, if He knew it would never work out right?" But the answer is clear. Judas was called by the Lord; he was destined to be a man of God. He was handpicked by the Saviour; he could have been mightily used by God. But Judas aborted God's plan. He broke the heart of Jesus. What started out as a beautiful, perfect plan of God ended in disaster, because Judas chose to go his own way. Pride and stubbornness wrecked the plan of God that was in operation.

So lay off all your guilt trips. Stop condemning yourself. Stop trying to figure out what you did wrong. It is what you are thinking right now that really counts with God. You did not make a mistake; more than likely, you simply gave too much. Like Paul, you have to say, "The more I loved, the less I was loved"(*see* 2 Corinthians 12:15).

Remind yourself God knows exactly how much you can take, and He will not permit you to reach a breaking point. Our loving Father said:

> There hath no temptation taken you but such as is common to man: but God is faithful, who will not suffer you to be tempted above that ye are able; but will with

the temptation also make a way to escape, that ye may be
able to bear it.

1 Corinthians 10:13

The worst kind of blasphemy is to think God is behind all
your hurt and pain, that it is the heavenly Father disciplining
you, that God thinks you need one or two more heartbreaks
before you are ready to receive His blessings. Not so!

It is true the Lord chastens those He loves. But that chastening is only for a season and is not meant to hurt us. God is
not the author of the confusion in your life; neither are you. It
is human failure. It is the enemy sowing tares in your field of
endeavor. It is the deception in someone else near you, who
lost faith in God. The enemy tries to hurt us through other
humans, just as he tried to hurt Job through an unbelieving
wife.

Your heavenly Father watches over you with an unwaver-
ing eye. Every move is monitored. Every tear is bottled. He
identifies with your every pain. He feels every hurt. He
knows when you have been exposed to enough harassment
from the enemy. He steps in and says, "Enough!" When the
hurt and pain no longer draw you closer to the Lord, when,
instead, it begins to downgrade your spiritual life, God moves
in. He will not permit a trusting child of His to go under
because of too much pain and agony of soul. When the hurting
begins to work to your disadvantage, when it begins to hinder
your growth, God must act and lift you out of the battle for a
while. He will never allow you to drown in your tears. He will
not permit your hurt to destroy your mind. He promises to
come, right on time, to wipe away your tears and give you joy
for mourning. God's word says: ". . . weeping may endure for
a night, but joy cometh in the morning" (Psalms 30:5).

**When you hurt the worst, go to your secret prayer closet and
weep out all your bitterness.**   Jesus wept. Peter wept bit-
terly! Peter carried with him the hurt of denying the very Son

of God. He walked alone on the mountains, weeping in sorrow. Those bitter tears worked a sweet miracle in him. He came back to shake the kingdom of Satan.

A woman who had endured a mastectomy wrote a book entitled *First You Cry*. How true! Recently I talked with a friend who was just informed he had terminal cancer. "The first thing you do," he said, "is cry until there are no more tears left. Then you begin to move closer to Jesus, until you know His arms are holding you tight."

Jesus never looks away from a crying heart. He said, "A broken heart will I not despise" (*see* Psalms 51:17). Not once will the Lord say, "Get hold of yourself! Stand up and take your medicine! Grit your teeth and dry your tears." No! Jesus bottles every tear in His eternal container.

Do you hurt? Bad? Then go ahead and cry! And keep on crying until the tears stop flowing. But let those tears originate only from hurt, and not from unbelief or self-pity.

Convince yourself you will survive, you will come out of it; live or die, you belong to the Lord. Life does go on. You would be surprised how much you can bear, with God helping you. Happiness is not living without pain or hurt—not at all. True happiness is learning how to live one day at a time, in spite of all the sorrow and pain. It is learning how to rejoice in the Lord, no matter what has happened in the past.

You may feel rejected. You may feel abandoned. Your faith may be weak. You may think you are down for the count. Sorrow, tears, pain, and emptiness may swallow you up, at times; but God is still on His throne. He is still God!

You can't help yourself. You can't stop the pain and hurt. But our blessed Lord will come to you, and He will place His loving hand under you and lift you up to sit again in heavenly places. He will deliver you from the fear of dying. He will reveal His endless love for you.

Look up! Encourage yourself in the Lord. When the fog

surrounds you and you can't see any way out of your dilemma, lie back in the arms of Jesus and simply trust Him. He has to do it all! He wants your faith, your confidence. He wants you to cry aloud, "Jesus loves me! He is with me! He will not fail me! He is working it all out, right now! I will not be cast down! I will not be defeated! I will not be a victim of Satan! I will not lose my mind or my direction! God is on my side! I love Him and He loves me!"

The bottom line is faith. And faith rests on this one absolute: "No weapon that is formed against thee shall prosper . . ." (Isaiah 54:17).

2

You Can't Carry Your Own Cross

It's very true that Jesus said to His disciples, ". . . If any man will come after me, let him deny himself, and take up his cross, and follow me" (Matthew 16:24). But Jesus could not carry His cross, and neither can you! Jesus fell under the load of His cross, weary, exhausted, and unable to carry it another step. John said, "And he bearing his cross went forth into a place called . . . Golgotha" (John 19:17). The Bible doesn't tell us how far Jesus carried His cross. We do know Simon of Cryrene was compelled to pick it up and carry it to the place of crucifixion (Matthew 27:32).

Jesus did take up His cross and was led by His tormentors, like a lamb to be slain. But He could not carry it for long. The truth is, Jesus was too weak and frail to carry His cross. It was laid on another's shoulders. He had reached the end of His endurance; He was a physically broken and wounded man. There is only so much one person can take. There is a breaking point.

Why did they compel Simon to pick up that cross? Was Jesus lying on that cobblestone street, like a lifeless man, with the cross lying over Him like dead weight? Did they kick

Him, try to prop Him up, and attempt to force Him a step
farther? And did He just lie there with not enough strength to
move an inch? His cross had become too heavy to bear.

What does this mean to us? Would our Lord make us do
something He could not do? Did He not say, "And whosoever
doth not bear his cross, and come, after me, cannot be my
disciple"? (Luke 14:27). A cross is a cross, be it wooden or
spiritual. It is not enough to say, "His cross was different; our
cross is spiritual."

Personally, it gives me great hope to know Jesus could not
take up His cross. It encourages me to know I am not the only
one burdened down to the ground at times, unable to go on
in my own strength. If we are going to identify with His
crucifixion, we must also identify with the steps that led to the
cross. We must face, once and for all, the truth that no human
being can carry his own cross.

Don't look for some hidden interpretation; Jesus knew
exactly what He was saying when He called us to take up our
crosses and follow Him. He remembers His cross. He remembers that another had to carry it for Him. Why, then,
would He ask us to shoulder crosses He knows will soon crush
us to the ground? He knows we can't carry them all the way in
our own strength. He knows all about the agony, the
helplessness, and the burden a cross creates.

There is a truth hidden here which we must uncover. It is a
truth so powerful and edifying, it could change the way we
look at all our troubles and hurts. Even though it almost
sounds sacrilegious to suggest Jesus did not carry His own
cross, that is the truth. What it means to us today is that Jesus,
who is touched by the feelings of our infirmities, must experience for Himself what it is like to be weak, discouraged, and
unable to go on without help. He was in all points tempted
just as we are. The temptation is not in failing or in laying
down the cross because of weakness. The real temptation is in

trying to pick up that cross and carrying it on in our own strength. God could have supernaturally lifted that cross and magically levitated it all the way to Calvary. Then, too, He could have taken the weight out of the cross and made it featherlike. But He did not. The crucifixion scene was not a series of blunders, and, though Christ died at the hands of sinners, the entire plan was borne in the heart of God from the foundation of the world. God put Simon there, ready to play his part in the plan of redemption. God was not caught by surprise when His Son could no longer carry the cross and thus fulfill prophecy. God knew Jesus would take up His cross, follow toward Golgotha, then lay it down.

Your Cross Is Meant to Bring You Down

God knows also that not one of His children can carry the cross he takes up when following Christ. We so much want to be good disciples; we so much want to deny ourselves and take the cross upon ourselves. We seem to forget that same cross will one day bring us to the end of our human strength and endurance. Would Jesus purposely ask us to take up crosses that He knows will sap all our human energies and leave us lying helpless—even to the point of giving up? Absolutely! Jesus forewarns us, ". . . without me ye can do nothing" (John 15:5). So He asks us to take up our crosses and struggle on with them, until we learn that lesson. Not until our crosses push us down into the dust, do we learn the lesson that it is not by our might nor power nor strength, but it is by His power. That is what the Bible means when it says His strength is made perfect in our weakness. It has never meant that God's way is a little better than ours or that His strength is a bit superior. It means that God's way is the only way; His strength is the only hope!

Jesus looks upon this world—filled with confused children

going about trying to establish their own righteousness and trying to please Him in their own ways—and He calls for crosses. The cross is meant to break us, to drain us of all human effort. We know we have One stronger than Simon who will come at our breaking point and take over the burden, but He cannot take over until we give up, until we come to that point where we cry, "God, I can't go another step. I'm exhausted! I'm broken! My strength is gone! I feel dead! Help!"

Jesus was crucified "through weakness" (2 Corinthians 13:4). It is when we become totally weak and self-abased that we witness the crucifixion of our own pride. Out of weakness we are made strong, by faith in the Lord. Our spirits are willing to carry our own crosses, but our flesh is weak. Paul could glory in his cross, taking pleasure in how weak it made him. He said:

> . . . I take pleasure in infirmities, in reproaches, in necessities, in persecutions, in distresses for Christ's sake: for when I am weak, then am I strong. And he said unto me, My grace is sufficient for thee: for my strength is made perfect in weakness. . . .
>
> 2 Corinthians 12:10,9

Paul was not weak and strong at the same time. He grew weak because of troubles and distresses. But when he was cast down to the ground by his cross, he did not despair. It was out of that weakness he became strong. Paul rejoiced in this process of being made weak, because it was the secret to his power with Christ. ". . . Most gladly therefore will I rather glory in my infirmities, that the power of Christ may rest upon me" (2 Corinthians 12:9).

What is your cross? It is any burden or pressure that threatens to break you down! My junkie friends call theirs "a monkey on the back." That is not a sacrilegious reference to the cross; it simply defines their image of a burden that crushes them to the ground. I have often heard husbands and wives refer to their marriages as their "cross to bear." Others see their cross as an unfulfilling job, an illness, a state of loneliness, or divorce. I have heard all kinds of definitions of what the cross is supposed to represent. I have even heard homosexuals refer to their habit as a heavy cross. Since Jesus did not describe the details of the cross we are to take up, I suggest it is anything that will hasten a crisis in our spiritual lives. For example, loneliness can be a cross, if it becomes a burden too heavy to bear and if it finally brings us to the end of ourselves. It is then we can allow the Lord to reach down to us and lift us out of our pity and self-destructiveness. Loneliness is a good thing, if it makes us weak enough to want only His strength.

"I'm not doing enough for God."   My cross is peculiar, but not unfamiliar to many others. I am constantly burdened by a sense of *never doing enough*. This cross usually becomes the heaviest right after I've written a best-selling book, after I've preached to thousands, after I've launched a feeding program for starving children, or after I've counseled with hundreds of troubled couples. I stop for a few weeks, take inventory of my life and ministry, and something in me gets restless. I get depressed and confess to my wife and friends, "I don't feel as if I'm doing anything for God. I'm not as fulfilled as I should be. Sometimes I feel so useless."

So often I get that "unfinished" feeling. I feel I'm wasting too much time doing insignificant things. It's hard to relax when a voice inside condemns me for not "burning out for Jesus." I think of all the things I promise myself I will do, the projects I'll finish, the growth in God I'll achieve, and much of it never gets done. I accuse myself of being lazy. Others seem to be so disciplined and motivated, and I picture them, in my mind, as passing me by, leaving me behind in the dust. But God will ask me to keep taking up that cross daily, until it finally gets the best of me. Evidently that's a part of my life that is not yet under His control. One day I'll fall down in despair and cry, "Lord, I just don't care anymore. Let the world pass me by. Let my dreams all fade. Let me be nothing but an obedient disciple. I don't want to compete with myself or others anymore. No more ego goals. Take over, Lord, and lift my load." That is when our Lord will step in and whisper, "Now, David, let Me carry your load."

Spiritual crosses. Sometimes spiritual pride can be a cross. You take on a heavy load when you begin to testify about the great things God is doing in your life. God gives you a broken and contrite spirit; others come to you for help, and they receive blessings; you are used in wonderful ways to encourage people all around you. It begins to dawn on you, "Wow! I've had such great joy. God has made me so tender and loving. I'm finally learning how to overcome my temptations, and I'm growing so much in the Lord. I feel as if I'm about to break through into a life of spiritual glory and power. At last I've reached a place of trust and peace. I don't ever want to go back to what I was."

A week later, you are groveling in the dust; your spiritual balloon burst, and everything seems to have drained out of you. All you can say is, "What happened? I haven't sinned against God; I haven't doubted. The joy just disappeared. I don't seem to have anything in me now to give to others. I'm dry and empty. Why couldn't I have kept the beautiful feelings?"

You Will Never *Arrive*

Hear me, friend. God will never permit you to feel as if you have arrived. That's the trouble with too many Christians

today. Way back, they received a great blessing from the
Lord. God did a wonderful work in their lives. The Holy
Spirit came upon them and redid their lives, through and
through. It was glorious, and they started telling the world
about their awakening. But it's been downhill ever since.
They have been riding out that one great experience and, in
the process, have become self-satisfied and complacent. Take
heed when you think you stand, lest you fall. Finally, that
once-blessed Christian ends up feeling weak and empty. After
trying, unsuccessfully, to invest and recreate the blessings, he
gives up in despair. He cries out, "I'm spiritually dead. I'm
losing ground with God. I feel like a phony. I can't seem to get
back to where I was in the Lord."

Your love for Jesus can put you on your knees, but your
cross will put you on your face—on the ground, in the dust.
God meets you in your prostrate condition and whispers, "I
have chosen the weak things of the world; the foolish things;
the broken things; the things that are nothing, that no flesh
should glory in His presence."

The Cross Teaches Us How to Deny Self

We will have to carry our crosses until we learn to deny.
Deny what? The one thing that constantly hinders God's work
in our lives: self. Look again at what Jesus said: "If any man
will come after me, let him deny himself, and take up his cross
and follow me." We are misinterpreting this message if we
emphasize self-denial, that is, the rejection of material or un-
lawful things. Jesus was not calling upon us to learn self-
discipline before we take up our cross. It is far more severe
than that. Jesus is asking that we deny ourselves. This means
to deny our own ability to carry any cross in our own strength.
In other words, "Don't take up your cross until you are ready
to reject any and every thought of becoming a holy disciple as
a result of your own effort."

There are millions of professing Christians who boast about their self-denial. They don't drink or smoke or curse or fornicate; they are examples of tremendous discipline. But not in a hundred years would they admit it was accomplished by anything other than their own willpower. In fact, they are quick to add statements like the following: "I can quit any time I want." "The devil can't trick me." "I know what's right and I try to do it." "I keep all the commandments." "I'm a clean, moral person." "I don't lie or cheat, and I am faithful to my marriage vows."

They are practicing self-denial, but they have never denied self. In some ways, we are all like that. We experience spurts of holiness, accompanied by feelings of purity. Good works usually produce good feelings. But God will not allow us to think our good works and clean habits can save us. That is why we need a cross.

I believe Jesus is actually saying to us, "Before you take up your cross, be ready to face a moment of truth. Be ready to experience a crisis by which you will learn to deny your self-will, your self-righteousness, your self-sufficiency, your self-authority. You can rise up and follow Me as a true disciple only when you can freely admit you can do nothing in your own strength. You cannot overcome sin through your own willpower. Your temptations cannot be overcome by your self-efforts alone. You cannot work things out by your own intellect."

Jesus Never Forces a Cross on Us

Jesus said, "Let *him* take up his cross." Never once does our Lord say, "Stoop down and let *Me* lay a cross on you." Jesus is not in the drafting business; His army is all volunteer. Not all Christians carry crosses. You can be a believer without carrying a cross, but you cannot be a disciple. I see so many believers rejecting the way of the cross. They have opted for the good life, with its prosperity, its material gain, its popularity and success. I'm sure many of them will make heaven— they will have saved their skins, but they will not have learned Christ. Having rejected the suffering and sorrow of the cross, they will not have the capacity to know and enjoy Him in eternity, as will all the cross-bearing saints who have entered into the fellowship of His suffering. Those who suffer will reign together.

I am not glorifying the suffering and pain—only the results they produce. Like Paul, we should look at the trials and hurts we are now experiencing and rejoice in the knowledge we are going down the only path that leads to ultimate victory and maturity. No longer, then, do we look at our burdens and troubles as accidents and penalties, but as crosses that are offered to teach us submission to God's way of doing things.

If you are hurting right now, you are in the process of healing. If you are down, crushed under the burden of a heavy load, get ready! God is about to show Himself strong on your behalf. You are at the point of revelation. At any time now, your Simon will appear, because God does use people to perform His will. Someone is going to be compelled by the Holy Spirit to come into your path of suffering, reach out to you, and help lift your burden.

Your Cross Is a Sign of His Love

Dear friend, don't think of your trial as judgment from God. Don't go about condemning yourself, as though you have brought down upon yourself some dreaded penalty for failure. Stop thinking, "God is making me pay for my sin." Why can't you see that what you are going through is a result of His love? Are you being chastened? Do you feel as if you are being dragged down? Are you in pain? Are you suffering? Good!

That is the evidence of His love toward you. Submit! Take up
your cross! Be prepared to go down even more. Get ready to
reach your crisis. Get ready to reach the end of yourself. Be
prepared to give up. Be prepared to hit bottom!

Please understand you are in Christ's own school of disci-
pleship. Rejoice that you are going to become weak in order
to experience His overpowering strength in you.

He laid His cross down; why won't you? For Him, a Simon
appeared. For us, a Saviour appears. We get up and go on.
It's still our cross, but now it's on His shoulders.

> Two are better than one; because they have a good
> reward for their labour. For if they fall, the one will lift
> up his fellow: but woe to him that is alone when he
> falleth; for he hath not another to help him up.
>
> Ecclesiastes 4:9, 10

3

You Can't Depend on
Others for Your Happiness

Recently a sad young minister and his wife came to me for counseling. After four troubled years of marriage, and two children, they were contemplating divorce. She was the saddest-looking wife I have seen in years. Her husband, the young youth minister, stood nearby, shuffling his weight from foot to foot, while his teary-eyed wife sobbed out her confession to me.

"There is absolutely no hope for our marriage now," she cried. "We are in two different worlds. He is so wrapped up in his work; he has no time left for me and the children. My whole world has been wrapped up in him; but now I'm getting tired of sitting home, waiting for him. I'm not accomplishing anything on my own. I don't even know if I love him anymore."

It hurt me to see such a lovely young couple acting like strangers to each other. I recognized the cause of their problem immediately: Both were bored, restless, and unhappy with each other. Just as multitudes of other couples, they once stood before a minister, to be married; they were gazing lovingly into each other's eyes, with their hearts filled with hope and anticipation that their marriage would be happy and

33

fulfilling. Now, just a few years later, their hopes are in ashes. They became disillusioned, and, try as they may, they can't seem to rekindle the spark of first love. It is then the ugly thoughts of divorce surface.

I looked that young wife in the eye and said, "What a shame that all your happiness depends only on what your husband does. If he is a good husband, if he treats you the way you think you should be treated, if he spends a little time with you—then you may find a little happiness. But when he lets you down, you have nothing left. Your whole world rises and falls on the actions of your husband. That is why you are so empty."

She nodded affirmatively, then bowed her head sheepishly while I continued. "Young lady, you're not a whole person. You're just half a person. You cannot survive if you depend on someone else for your happiness. True women's liberation means finding your own happiness, in yourself, through God's power. You must become your own person and quit depending on your husband, or someone else, to make you happy."

She knew I was right—I had hit the nail right on the head. She promised to change her way of thinking and get involved with life, herself. I left them, convinced she was determined to step out of her role as an emotional cripple and find her own source of happiness through a new relationship with God.

The True Cause of Divorce and Broken Relationships

Husbands and wives are becoming emotional cripples who lean all over each other, causing both to fall. We mess up our relationships because we live under the influence of a lie. We have convinced ourselves we have a right to happiness and that our spouses are morally obligated to create it for us. The danger of that lie is that when we can't find the happiness we expect from them, we put all the blame on their failure to do what was right.

Our divorce courts today are overcrowded with husbands and wives seeking divorce simply on the grounds that their marriage gives them no happiness. One such divorced husband told me, "God bless my dear wife; she tried so hard. I gave that woman three of the best years of my life, hoping she could learn to understand me and make me feel like a man. She just didn't have it in her. She simply did not know how to make me happy."

That man will probably get married once or twice again, hoping a new wife will succeed where the first one failed. Some keep marching down the aisle with one new partner after another, trying desperately to find one understanding soul mate who will create happiness for them. But they seldom find it. Their misery and unhappiness increase with each new marriage partner.

No other human being on earth can create happiness for you. You must create it for yourself through the work of God in your own life. Marriage is not made up of two halves trying to become a whole. Rather, marriage consists of two whole people who are bridged by the Spirit of God. Marriage never works unless each party maintains his or her own identity, settles his own values, finds his own sense of fulfillment, and discovers his own source of happiness. Each must be complete, in himself, through the Lord.

Why allow what someone else does to destroy your life? Why permit the actions of another to rob you of your peace and joy? Why can't you be your own person? Why can't you look life right in the eye and say, "From now on, I'll not allow someone else to drag me down. I am determined to be a whole person, and I will discover my own source of happiness. No more leaning on someone else to give meaning and purpose to my life! I want a happiness that will not be lost just because somebody fails me."

Step Out of Your Bondage to the Actions of Others

I say to every housewife who will hear me: "Step out of your bondage of living your life only through others." God never intended that you find happiness only through your husband or your children. I am not suggesting that you forsake them, only that you forsake your degrading bondage to the idea that your happiness depends only on other people. God wants you to discover a life of true happiness and contentment, based only on what you are as a person and not on the moods and whims of people around you.

Wives who become clinging vines are not attractive to intelligent men. Husbands eventually walk all over wives who lean on them and exude an attitude that suggests, "You are my whole world, and if you ever let me down, I might as well kill myself." Wives who become independently happy and content in and with themselves suddenly become mystifyingly attractive. The truly attractive wife is the one who can say to her husband, "I love you, and I'll be your friend, but I'm a person, too. I'm going to act like a whole person, and my happiness will be what I create through my own relationship with God."

This is also a message that every young person must heed to survive the pressures of broken relationships so common today. How can young people find happiness when their parents are splitting up and their homes are disintegrating? They, too, need to learn not to depend on others for their happiness.

A nineteen-year-old girl confessed, "My dad and mom have been in love for over twenty-three years. I think theirs is just about a perfect marriage. If I ever learned they had been having problems and were putting on a good front just for me, I think I'd die. In fact, if my folks ever got a divorce, I'd go out and do drugs, sex, and alcohol, just to get even with them. I'd throw my life away."

"What a horrible concept," I told her. "Isn't it a shame that all your happiness depends on what your parents do? If they fail, so does your purpose in life. You will go all through life substituting others in the place of your parents. You will always have to have an idol—someone to be your good example. You will never be your own person. You will fail only because someone else fails you. What a pity!"

Our young people today must learn to find their own sources of happiness; they must no longer depend on their parents to create it for them. Thank God I am now meeting hundreds of young people who have found their own places of happiness in the Lord. One young man told me, "I love my parents, but I'm not going to allow their divorce to affect me. I'm going on with God. I have my own life to live, and I'm not going to let them drag me down by their actions."

We must give ourselves to the needs of others. We must help heal the hurts of those we love. We must get under one another's burdens, but we can do all of this only when we are happy with ourselves. We can help others find themselves only after we have found ourselves in the Lord.

There Is a Right Way to Find Happiness

I'm not one who cares much for formulas or how-to directions. But in my own experience, I have found a simple way to find a true happiness that does not depend on what others do. It is a happiness that does not come and go, and it is not affected by the moods, words, or actions of people in my life—even those I love the most.

What is that secret? *I have discovered that my needs are spiritual, not physical!* Our basic human needs include food, water, shelter, and the air we breathe. Beyond that, our needs are spiritual. And those needs can't be met by any human being.

All unhappiness is a result of trying to meet our needs through human relationships. When another human being fails to meet our needs, we become frustrated and unhappy. For example, the husband comes home from work tired, short-tempered, and feeling a need for a kind, understanding word from his wife. He is depressed, and he wants his wife to make him feel better. In turn, his wife has her own needs. She is feeling down, lonely, and she is wanting him to lift her spirits. So they lean on each other. The unspoken message rings out, "I'm hurting, honey, heal me. I'm down, lift me up. I'm depressed, make me happy. I'm blue, take my blues away. I'm in need, meet that need. Put your arms around me and love all the hurt out of me."

Of course, neither of them can meet the needs in the other, because those needs are spiritual, and only God can meet them. You can be in the arms of someone you love all night long and still wake up crying inside. The discovery is soon made that those needs cannot be met by sex or by a tender word. That is why some men pay a prostitute one hundred dollars a night, just to sit up and talk with them. They hope their blues can be talked away. It never works, because the next night they are seeking someone else to share their problems with.

We expect our spouses to do Godlike work. We expect miracles of them. We know only that we have overwhelming needs and that they must be met.

I have had lonely people tell me, "If only God would give me someone to love, I'd be such a better person and a better Christian. I know all my unhappiness is a result of being so alone all the time. I need a friend; only then will I be truly happy."

I say, "Not so!" Another person, male or female, may give you temporary relief from the agony of loneliness; but, unless you are a whole person, with your own source of inner strength, the old feelings of despair and loneliness will once again overwhelm you.

Two years ago, my wife and I counseled a young lady who insisted she was the loneliest girl in the state of Texas. She said, "If I could only find a husband, get married, and settle down, I'd never be lonely again." We helped pray in her prince charming. She did get married to a fine young Christian gentleman. But three months after the wedding, she was back to us in tears, crying, "I'm still lonely. I'm still empty. I know now it wasn't just the man I needed. I haven't settled things in my own life yet." That girl will never be a good wife until she learns to quit leaning on other people to meet her needs.

A young divorcée asked my wife and me to pray that her estranged husband would return. She was nearly hysterical, crying, "I want him back so badly. I know I messed up our marriage—I was so crazy and immature. But now that he's gone, I want him back. I think I've grown up. I've matured. I know I can do it right this time, but he's been dating another woman. I'm so desperate that if God won't bring him back to me soon, I'm going to go out to the nearest bar and tag on the biggest drunk you ever saw."

I informed her we would not pray for his return, because she was not ready for him. She would mess it up all over again. Why? Because she was still not a whole person. She was ready to throw her morals away if he did not come home to try once again to make her happy. That is why many people don't get such prayers answered. They are not ready to try again. They would make the same mistakes all over again, even if remarried to someone else. They are still leaning on others, always using someone else as a crutch to hold them up. They have not become whole persons, and they are not complete in themselves.

God Alone Is the Only Source of All Happiness and Contentment

Paul said, ". . . my God shall supply all your need according to his riches in glory by Christ Jesus" (Philippians 4:19). Not your husband or your wife, pastor, psychiatrist, or your best friend—but God! Go ahead and share your problems with your friend or pastor or a professional counselor. But, in the final analysis, they can help you only if they make you face yourself. You must do it on your own—take your needs to the Lord and allow Him to make you whole. Eventually, you must get rid of every crutch and lean completely on Jesus alone.

When your relationship with the Lord is wrong, it affects all human relationships. Most Christian married couples are not having trouble with their marriages. Rather, they are having trouble with God, with faith, with prayer; therefore, they have trouble with each other.

When people confess to me that their marriages are in trouble, I don't have to dig too deeply until I discover they are not where they should be with the Lord. They are bored with the things of God, so they are bored with life and marriage. They have lost touch with God and, in turn, have lost touch with their spouses. These husbands and wives are not really suffering from a lack of communication with each other; they are suffering mostly from a lack of communication with God. When people quit talking to God, they quit talking to one another. And people who quit talking to God soon get very lonely and depressed. They are actually lonely for God, hungering for communion with Him, yearning for His close love and nearness; but, instead of recognizing these needs as spiritual, they blame their lack of fulfillment on their husbands or wives.

If most Christians were truly honest, they would have to admit there is nothing terminal about their marriage problems. What is wrong is their relationship to the Lord. Their faith is in trouble, and when people are not on right terms with God, they get frustrated and take it out on the ones they love the most. They are actually angry with themselves. That empty, restless feeling is a hunger for God. But instead of returning to the secret closet to satisfy that thirst, most Christians drift farther away and fall deeper into despair.

There is not a Christian in this world, who, deep in his heart, is not aware that God will help him. We know God can heal all our hurts; we know He can heal any marriage; we know He can wipe away every tear and bring joy. But we simply do not take the time or effort to run to Him in our hour of need.

You can be happy. You can be a whole person, and you need never again lean on another human being. That is not to say we don't need one another. We need the prayer, help, and comfort of loving friends and family. But there can be no lasting happiness if we expect others to create it for us.

Why not allow Him to renew your heart, renew a right spirit in you, and reveal to you that in His presence there is fullness of joy and pleasures evermore? That is why Jesus said, ". . . Be of good cheer. . . . Lo, I am with you alway . . ." (Matthew 14:27; 28:20).

4

Have You Felt Like Giving Up Lately?

A growing number of ministers have been writing to me, in recent months, telling of their concern for parishioners who are simply giving up. One minister wrote:

> I see my church members trying so hard to cope with problems in their marriages and pressures in their personal lives. Just when it seems victory is within reach, they stumble and fall. Good, honest Christians are so often overwhelmed by guilt and condemnation; it causes despair. When they can't live up to their own expectations, when they fall back into sin and get involved, they decide to give up. Few know how to pull out of a moral tailspin.

I agree with the assessment of these ministers. Growing numbers of Christians *are* at the breaking point. None of the talk about giving up has to do with the Lord. Few Christians would even dare entertain thoughts of quitting on their love for Jesus. Most despairing Christians think only of giving up on themselves. You hear it so often, "I just can't go on anymore. I can't make it, even though I try so hard. It's hopeless. Why try?"

I hear some ministers today who continually preach only a positive message. To hear them tell it, every Christian is receiving miracles; everybody is getting instant answers to prayer; everybody is feeling good, living good, and the whole world is bright and rosy. I love to hear that kind of preaching, because I really desire all those good and healthy things for God's people. But that's not the way things are for a great number of very honest, sincere Christians. How sad to hear such shallow theology being pushed from pulpits today. It's an insult to a lowly Jesus who became poor, who died a failure in the eyes of the world. It is this kind of materialistic preaching that has so ill prepared an entire generation to endure any kind of pain, to be content with such things as they have, to be abased and not always abounding. Serving God becomes a kind of Olympic race, in which everyone must strive for the gold medals.

No wonder our young people give up in defeat. They can't live up to the image, created by religion, of a happy-go-lucky, rich, successful, always positive-thinking Christian. Their world is not that idealistic. They look in a mirror reflecting a face covered with ugly pimples. They live with heartbreaks, hour-by-hour crises, and horrible family problems. Their friends are hooked and dying on all sides. They look into the uncertain future, frightened and worried. Loneliness, fear, and depression hound them daily.

Positive thinking won't make their problems go away. Confessing these problems don't really exist doesn't change a thing. These apostles of the positive dare not exclude the Gethsemane experiences of life. The cup of pain, the hour of isolation, and the night of confusion were all part of the Master's life-style. Our great achievements and our successes ought to take place at Gethsemane, not Fort Knox.

The sawdust trail for many has become the gold-dust trail.

The Bible has become a catalog, with unlimited order blanks for life's goodies for everyone who wants to become a "silver" saint. Anything having to do with Job-like pain and suffering is considered negative living.

God is good, and those who give generously do receive abundant blessings. One should always think on good and honest reports; but pain, poverty, and suffering have befallen some of the saintliest of God's people, just as they did righteous Job.

What do you say to that wife whose home is breaking up, while she seems powerless to stop it? She's been advised by her friends, counseled by her pastor, and exhorted over and over again, "Stay on your knees and believe God for a miracle." So she fasts, and she prays. She bends over backwards to the point of crawling on her knees to her husband. She exercises faith with every intellectual insight she possesses. But, in spite of all her honest efforts, he grows hard and bitter, demanding a divorce. Not all marriages are healed through prayer or good intentions. It takes two to make a marriage work, and even though prayer may bring the power of Holy Ghost conviction upon a straying mate, that mate can resist all of God's efforts and abort the solution.

Some of my friends may be wondering why I am spending so much time talking about marriage, divorce, and the home. The reason is simple enough: In my crusades I talk to so many kids on the brink of suicide, and an overwhelming majority tell me their depression stems from trouble at home. Dad and Mom are having trouble, or they have already gotten a divorce.

Multitudes of husbands and wives are giving up on their marriages. A minister friend of mine, whose divorce had just become final, told me he has become a hero of sorts to some of his closest friends. One friend called him and asked, "Where did you get the courage to split up? Man, we're having trouble, too, but I guess I'm a coward. Wish I could take that step."

Another called, saying, "Our marriage is a farce. We don't communicate at all anymore. I've given up. But how do you take that final plunge into divorce? I'm so hung up on security and my job; I'm just afraid I'd lose too much."

Still another called and offered, "I admire your courage. You got out of a hopeless situation. I guess I'll go on existing, living in misery. I don't want my kids to turn on me; that's the only thing holding me. I've given up completely on our marriage."

There are many of you who, at this very moment, are on the verge of giving up. You can't understand what is happening to you, to your marriage, to your home. Something is missing; and, try as you will, you simply cannot find the key to make things work out right. How many hours have you spent all alone, trying to figure out where things went wrong? The magic is gone. The romance is gone. The communication is gone. In their places now are arguments, questions, suspicions, innuendoes, cutting remarks.

A brokenhearted lady wrote:

> Sir, I just can't believe it's happening to me. I was so secure, feeling sorry for all those others who seemed to be having so many problems. Never did I imagine our marriage could crumble. I was too intelligent, too much into giving and sharing. Now I'm a victim of this curse of divorce. It's a shattering experience.

A successful marriage counselor took me to lunch recently and before the entree was served, he confessed his own marriage had been in jeopardy. "You just can't take any good marriage for granted anymore," he said. "I find I have to work harder than ever to keep a good thing. I'm convinced Satan is determined to break up my marriage and every good Christian marriage. It's a well-planned attack on the best of marriages. If Satan can get the strongest, most-admired marriages broken up, the weaker ones will be tempted to quit struggling and give up."

The secret struggles in the Christian's personal life are just as critical. The inner battles of the average Christian today are staggering in intensity and proportion. Multitudes are involved in situations too hard to comprehend. Like David, the Psalmist, they confessed, "My sins have overwhelmed me; they are too high for me to understand."

Paul said, "For we that are in this tabernacle do groan, being burdened . . ." (2 Corinthians 5:4). I doubt we could even count the great numbers of Christians who groan in secret, because of the burdens they carry.

Paul talked about trouble: ". . . trouble which came to us . . . we were pressed out of [burdened beyond] measure, above strength, insomuch that we despaired even of life" (2 Corinthians 1:8).

If you pulled back the facade from every great preacher and every admired personality, you would find moments of deep depression. You would find the same infirmities you find in any normal Christian. We all have seasons of despair, accompanied by feelings of failure. At times we have all thought of quitting. We have all had thoughts of giving up.

Why Do We Feel This Way?

Why do we feel like giving up at times? Mostly because we act as if God has forsaken the earth. We don't doubt His existence or His reality, but our prayers seem to go unanswered. We cry out for His help, in such desperation, and He seems not to hear. We struggle along, making one mistake after another. We make promises to do better; we get into the Bible; we cry and pray and stay busy helping others and doing good. But we are so often left with an empty, unfulfilled sensation. The promises of God haunt us. We claim those promises in what we believe is honest, childlike faith, but time after time we fail to receive what we ask for. In the hour of temptation, down we go!

Doubt creeps in, and Satan whispers, "Nothing works. Faith in God doesn't produce results. In spite of your tears, prayers, and trust in God's Word, nothing really changes. Days, weeks, and even years go by, and your prayers, hopes, and dreams are still unanswered and unfulfilled. Quit! Give up!"

Every Christian on this planet reaches that crisis point at one time or another in life. And in that moment, when the walls seem to be caving in and the roof appears to be collapsing, when everything seems to be coming apart and sin demands the upper hand, a voice deep within cries out, "Walk away from it all. Pack it in! Escape! Why put up with it? Run away. You don't have to take it. Do something drastic."

David, overwhelmed by the evil in his heart, cried out:

> Awake, why sleepest thou, O Lord? arise, cast us not off for ever. Wherefore hidest thou thy face, and forgettest our affliction and our oppression?
>
> Psalms 44:23, 24

Christian, does it amaze you that great men of God faced the same battles you and I face today? The Bible says:

> Beloved, think it not strange concerning the fiery trial which is to try you, as though some strange thing happened unto you: But rejoice, inasmuch as ye are partakers of Christ's sufferings; that, when his glory shall be revealed, ye may be glad also with exceeding joy.
>
> 1 Peter 4:12, 13

Job was a perfect man, in God's sight; yet he, too, experienced a time when he wanted to give up. Job's agony came from a terrible dilemma. He was convinced, in his heart, that God knew where he was and what he was going through; yet he could not enter into the presence of God. He lamented:

> Behold, I go forward, but he is not there; and backward, but I cannot perceive him: On the left hand, where he doth work, but I cannot behold him: he hideth himself on the right hand, that I cannot see him.
>
> Job 23:8, 9

Job was saying to himself, "I know God is there someplace, looking down on me in all my trouble. He knows the way I take; but, in spite of all I do to find Him, He keeps hiding from me. I believe God is real; He is there; but I just can't see Him." In total desperation, Job sobs: ". . . I am afraid of him. . . . The Almighty troubleth me" (Job 23:15, 16).

All those fearful and troubled thoughts about God were the result of what Job thought was a divine do-nothingness. Job argues that God doesn't cut him off, yet He doesn't remove the darkness (*see* Job 23:17).

The bottom line for Job was simply this: Either cut me down or make things right; just don't be silent toward me. Even if You cut me off, at least I'll know You are there.

What Is the Cure?

How can we learn to hold on and live one day at a time? You can begin by forgetting all shortcuts and magic cures. The Christian doesn't need a supposed demon of despair cast out, as if his going would make life easier. Nor will God come down and do our living for us. The tempter will not be destroyed until that day God casts him into prison. Satan will always be here, deceiving, accusing, and trying to rob every believer of his faith.

The longer I live for Christ, the more difficult it is for me to accept easy, cure-all solutions. In my own struggles I've found great comfort and help in two wonderful absolutes.

God really loves me!   This is the first absolute. God is not in the business of condemning His children—failures or not. He yearns over us as a loving Father, wanting only to lift us out of our weaknesses.

Recently I caught a glimpse of that love, while walking in the woods around our ranch. Not once did I stop to consider the birds flying about, free and healthy. But suddenly, there on the ground just ahead, flopped a crippled little bird. Struggling so hard to fly, the little baby bird could only flip over helplessly in the dust. I stooped to pick it up. It was then a familiar Scripture came flashing through my mind: ". . . and one [sparrow] . . . shall not fall on the ground without your Father" (Matthew 10:29).

I once thought that verse read, "Not a sparrow falls to the ground without the Father knowing about it." But Matthew's version states: "One shall not fall without the Father."

God is with us even when we fall. We do not fall without the Father. He does not fall into our sin, but He does come down to our fallen condition. He does not abandon us on our way down. He never forsakes a crippled child. For, you see, we are that sparrow.

David said, "I watch, and am as a sparrow alone upon the house top" (Psalms 102:7). David saw the bathing Bathsheba from that housetop, and he fell, a broken, crippled sparrow. But God did not give up on him. Our Lord never gives up on any of us.

Have you also fallen? Do you relate to that crippled sparrow, flopping helplessly in the dust? Are you wounded, hurting, and feeling lost and lonely? Do you ever think to yourself, "How can God put up with someone like me? How can He still love me when I've failed Him so badly"?

Oh, but He does love you, my friend. Often we can recognize His great love only when we have hit bottom and find ourselves in such need of it. You will have won a great victory if you can be convinced God loves you even in your wounded, crippled condition. It was a wound that made me kneel and show compassion for a helpless bird. And it is our wounds, our hurts, our helplessness which cause His love and compassion to overshadow and envelop us. Our strength is renewed by His everlasting love. Just rest in that wonderful love. Don't panic. Deliverance will come. God answers us by showing His love. When we have learned how weak we are and have learned to trust His love and forgiveness, He will stoop down and gently help us back to the nest.

It is my faith that pleases Him the most.　　The second absolute is this. ". . . without faith it is impossible to please him . . ." (Hebrews 11:6). ". . . Abraham believed God, and it was counted unto Him for righteousness."

God wants so much to be trusted. That trust He counts as righteousness. I know some very holy, sanctified people (at least outwardly) who walk the straight and narrow. They would never once admit to feelings of failure and despair. They think of themselves as saints; but their great sin is doubt. Sometimes I think certain sinners have more faith than many self-righteous Christians.

What do I do when temptation rolls over me like a flood? What do I do when my inadequacies overwhelm me, and I see the reflections of my weaknesses? Do I give up? Quit? Never! I bring to God all I have left: my faith in Him! I may not understand why He seems to take such a long time to intervene, but I know He will. He will keep His word to me.

I am convinced Satan wants to rob me of only one thing, and that is my faith. He really doesn't want my morals or my good deeds or my dreams. He wants to destroy my faith and make me believe God has forsaken this earth.

A fall is never fatal to those who keep their faith intact. In spite of continual struggles and feelings of helplessness, at times, I still believe my Lord. In spite of despair and pressures that stunt the mind and sap the strength, I believe God. I believe He will keep me from falling and present me faultless before the throne of glory, with exceeding great joy.

He loves me, and He wants me to keep on trusting; so I will accept that love, and keep my faith strong. "Thou wilt keep him in perfect peace, whose mind is stayed on thee: because he trusteth in thee" (Isaiah 26:3).

5

Are You Going Through a Dry Spell?

I preach to thousands, yet there are times I feel so very dry, so far away from the warm presence of God. In these moments of dryness, I have no great yearning to read the Word; my reading of the Bible is done mostly through a sense of obligation. When I'm dry and empty, I feel little compulsion to pray. I know my faith is intact, and my love for Jesus is strong. There is no desire in me to taste the things of this world. It's just that I can't seem to touch God in those days and weeks of spiritual dryness.

Have you ever sat in church and watched those all around you getting blessed, while you feel nothing? They cry; they pray; they worship with tremendous feelings. But you are not moved upon at all. You begin to wonder if there is something wrong with your spiritual life. Christians all around you are telling great stories about how God is blessing them and answering all their prayers. They seem to live on a mountain-top of happy experiences, while you just plod along, loving Jesus but not setting the world on fire. Some of your prayers still have not been answered. You don't shout or put on an emotional display. You have no big stories to tell about some fantastic miracle you've witnessed. It almost makes you feel like a second-class believer.

I believe all true believers experience dry spells at various times in their Christian lives. Even Jesus felt the isolation when He cried aloud: "Father, why have you forsaken me?"

Notes From My Diary, During a Dry Spell

I keep notes of almost every thought I receive in my nighttime devotions. Recently, during a dry spell, I recorded my feelings. I think there are many Christians who will relate to these honest notations made in my diary.

A note of caution before reading this very personal confession: When I talk about the sin in my own life, do not try to interpret that as some hideous, openly flaunted weakness. To me, whatever is not of faith is sin. We have all sinned and fallen short of the glory of God. I often fall into the gross sin of doubt. So please do not read into my confession of sin something not intended. Think of your own sin as you read.

> I wonder why God seems to be so distant at times. Is He angry with me? Does He have to hide from me because of failure in my life? Is God holding back on me in some way, bound by a contract in His Holy Word that demands He close His eyes in my direction, because of my stubbornness?
>
> Does sin cause a separation? Is God really there, wanting to break through to me with overwhelming joy and peace, but unable to, because of a barrier I have constructed as a result of a besetting sin? Must He hide against His will because He honors His Word above His name? He hid from Israel in times of backsliding. Must He hide from me for a while, until I see the horror of my sins and run from them?
>
> Does He finally get weary of my constant falling, and must He shut me off for a while only because He loves

me so? Does His omnipotent love demand He isolate me from His presence, until I break and yield, as a submitting child, weary of my emptiness and despair?

Or is all of this dryness a result of my own blindness? Is it just a result of living on feelings? Is He there, all the time, in spite of my failure, waiting for me to accept His forgiveness? Do I feel isolated only because I'm ashamed and burdened with guilt? Do I shun Him because I know I'm unworthy of His blessings? Has the knowledge of my weaknesses made me believe I have no right to expect this nearness and comfort?

I am not morbid; I have no death wish. It's not just the nighttime blues. I never once doubt my eternal salvation. What I do doubt is my ability to understand how God works. I have always felt the power of His great love. Even in my driest hours, the sense of His love for me is almost overwhelming. It is not enough to know the Father loves you; it is not enough to believe all His promises; it is not enough to walk in faith; it is not enough to know you want the Lord with all that is in you. There must be more.

There must be the nearness of the Lord, the still small voice and the joy of hearing that voice. There must be the knowledge that He not only abides, but that His Word is even in your mouth. The heart must feel His warmth. The flow of God's presence must fill the room. The tears that are all bottled up inside must find release. The joy of Jesus must rush through all the corridors of your mind. The heart must know He has come to guide, comfort, and help in the hour of need. There must be no doubt, no question that God has chosen to come and commune with His servant.

Without the nearness of God, there can be no peace. The dryness can be stopped only with the dew of His glory. The despair can be dispelled only by the assurance God is answering. The fire of the Holy Ghost must heat the mind, body, and soul.

I want God's total presence. I want to flow in His river of love. I want complete forgiveness of all my sins, but more than forgiveness, I want freedom. What is forgiveness without freedom? I know the Lord has promised to forgive me seven times in a single day. I know His love and forgiveness are to all generations. I know if I confess my sins, He is faithful and just to forgive and to cleanse me. But it is not enough to be forgiven and cleansed from yesterday's sins. I need freedom from the power of the sin that so easily besets me, freedom from the slavery of all passions, freedom from the chains of all iniquity.

I know God's Word promises freedom. I know the many Scriptures which talk of walking in the Spirit to avoid fulfilling the lusts of the flesh. I know about the warnings to flee all lusts. Other Scriptures flood my mind about overcoming the world, but there are times I don't seem to find the key. How do these verses work in a practical way in my everyday life? What does it really mean to walk in the Spirit? Does that mean you will never fall again? A child keeps falling while learning to walk. Adults stumble and fall. Can you fall, even while walking in the Spirit, then get up and walk again, getting stronger as you go?

God, You've got to be there! If You are not there in my time of dryness, there is no hope. You must be there, calling for me, longing for my voice, yearning over me as a father pities his child. If not, life has no meaning.

He cannot give up on me when I'm hurting. Yes, my flesh is weak. Yes, I fail Him over and over again. Yes, I've told Him how sorry I am a thousand times a year. Yes, I've promised to forsake the world and everything in it, but, at times, I can't seem to keep my word. Yes, there are a few times I feel like the worst kind of sinner, a cheat, a cad, a two-timing, worthless child. Yes, I do feel I am unworthy to ever expect Him to come near me when I feel so cheap and ungrateful.

But, in spite of all that, somehow I know He is not far off. Somehow I hear a distinct, small voice calling, "Come, My child. I am aware of all you are experiencing. I still love you. I will never leave you nor forsake you. We will face it together. I am still your Father, and you are My child. Come, not on your merits or goodness, but come on the merits of your Saviour, Jesus the Lord."

Somehow I know He will bring me out of this dry spell. I have in me a flame that will not be smothered. I seem to know the promises will be fulfilled. In His time, in His way, He will turn my dryness into a river of love. His Word will come to me. I will receive a new revelation of His will, a renewed spirit, and a greater peace of mind, all because He has never failed me once before.

Oh, God! I have feet of clay. My mind is strong in faith. My heart melts for You. My tears are hot with desire for the touch of the Lord, but my feet keep taking me astray. I am not walking in the Spirit, as I would honestly like to. Where is that day-by-day victory? Where is the power to keep myself holy and pure?

God, I search the Scripture, hoping to find a formula, a way out of the bondage of sin. If it means staying on my knees all night, then I'll do it. Does it mean reading my Bible through, until I stumble on a clear message of deliverance? Then I'll read and read! Most of the clichés and easy solutions offered by preachers do not work, even though they sound pious.

Somewhere there has to be victory over all the power of the enemy. Somewhere I can put aside the weight, the burden, the harassment. God promises total freedom, total victory over the power of the enemy. Someday my foot will no longer be snared in Satan's trap. Someday I'll look into my heart and see only Jesus, only holiness, only those things pleasing to God.

Someday God must lead all His children to a place of freedom from sin's power. The Word of God is so vast; I know so little of how to find in it the answers to my personal needs. The only hope is the Holy Spirit, who will supernaturally lead me to the truth that will set me free. I can't find it by myself. I can't get it out of books or from counselors. I can't understand any of it without the Holy Spirit revealing it to me. I want to know what God expects of me; I want to know how much is my part and how much is His!

Oh, God! Cleanse my desires. Make me desire those things You know to be best for me. If You gave me everything I desired, it would be a bedlam of confusion, with no order or harmony left. All my human desires are blind. They are usually out of keeping with my real needs and are often contrary to God's moral laws.

It is so easy to desire what would cause the greatest damage to myself, lead to the worst misery, and bring on the most tragic kind of confusion. I think of my desires as being well thought out, intelligent, and needful to my well-being.

Sin causes my desires to be loosed from God's moral law. They end up as foamings of the inner appetites. Soul hunger, aspirations, lusts, and passions reek with all kinds of disorder. They are phantoms without perception.

Where do many of my desires originate? Not from a spring of reason and common sense, but they are instigated, instead, by raw lustings of the old nature. They rush out of my mind like wild troops, confused, blind, and in total disarray. They swarm like bees, fast and wild.

As time goes by, I so often discover how vain and foolish my desires were. I desired to undertake a new project, and it exploded before I could get started. Later, I learned my disappointment was a blessing in disguise. If God had not interfered and kept those desires from me, I could have destroyed myself.

My desires can often be very morally bad. They can be fouled by lust. There is an entire breed of desires lurking beneath the surface, constantly pushed upon us all by our Adam nature, always breaking into the mind, mingling with our deepest and holiest thoughts. These evil desires seek to identify with our best thoughts, trying to make the mind accept them as God's thoughts.

Very often my personal desires are so dominant, so deeply imbedded, that they invade my mind in the secret closet. They become so powerful and persistent, I allow them to deceive me into accepting them as the still small voice of God in the inner man. May God keep me from the deception of my own immoral desires!

What Shall I Do to
Overcome Spiritual Dryness?

I must maintain a life of prayer.   Why is it none of us pray as we should, anymore? We know God is wanting to comfort and help us. We know our burdens can all be lifted when we are shut in with Him. There is something deep within us that keeps calling us to prayer. It is the voice of the Holy Spirit saying, "Come!" Come to the water that satisfies that soul thirst. Come to the Father, who pities His children. Come to the Lord of life, who promises to forgive every sin committed. Come to the One who refuses to condemn you or forsake you or hide from you.

God does not hide from us when we sin. Never! That is only our fear condemning our hearts. God did not hide in the garden, when Adam and Eve sinned. He still came to them, calling and yearning for their fellowship and love. We, ourselves, hide because of our guilt and condemnation. We can't imagine God still loving us when we are so disobedient and ungrateful.

Come boldly to His throne of grace, even when you have sinned and failed. He instantly forgives those who repent with godly sorrow. You don't have to spend hours and days in remorse and guilt. You don't have to earn your way back into His good graces. You don't have to pretend a superficial kind of sorrow or feign tears. Go to the Father, bend your knees, open your heart, and cry out your agony and pain. Tell Him all about your failings, all about your struggles. Tell Him about your loneliness, feelings of isolation, fears, and failures.

We try everything except prayer. We read books, looking for formulas and guidelines. We go to friends, ministers, and counselors, looking everywhere for a word of comfort or advice. We seek mediators and forget the one Mediator who has the answer to everything.

We don't pray, because it's so hard to do—most of the time. It's not hard when trouble comes unexpectedly, or when cancer strikes, or when a loved one suddenly dies of a heart attack. At these times we are so broken in spirit that we cry and pray. That's all right, but we should be leaning on Jesus through the good and the bad. We should be getting our strength and help long before the crisis overwhelms us. We should be pouring out our hearts to Him, every day of our lives.

No wonder we are so dry and empty. We have simply neglected the secret closet of prayer. It is not really dryness; it is lukewarmness. It is a growing coldness, caused by drifting along, getting away from the holy place.

Nothing dispels dryness and emptiness more quickly than an hour or two shut in with God. Putting off that date with God in His secret closet causes guilt. We know our love for Him should lead us into His presence; but we busy ourselves in so many other things, then time slips away, and God is left out. We throw in His direction a whole array of "thought prayers." But nothing can take the place of that secret closet with the door shut, praying to the Father in that seclusion. That is the solution to every dry spell.

I must no longer be afraid of a little suffering. Christ's Resurection was preceded by a short period of suffering. We do die! We do suffer! There is pain and sorrow!

We do not want to suffer or resist or be hurt. We want painless deliverance. We want· supernatural intervention. "Do it, God," we pray, "because I am weak and always will be. Do it all while I go my way, waiting for a supernatural deliverance." Or we blame our troubles on demons! We seek out a man of God and hope he can cast the demon out, so we can go our way with no pain or suffering. All done! Breeze right through to a peaceful life of victory. We want someone to lay hands on us and drive away all the dryness. But victory is not always without suffering and pain. Look at your sin. Face it. Suffer it through, as Jesus did. Fill up His suffering. Enter into it. Suffering endures only for a night, but joy always follows in the morning.

God sets before you a choice. His love demands a choice. If God supernaturally lifted us out of every battle, without pain or suffering, it would abort all trials and all temptation; there would be no free choice and no testing as by fire. It would be God superimposing His will on mankind. He chooses to meet us in our dryness and show us how it can become the way into a new life of faith.

It is often according to the will of God to suffer dryness and even pain: "Wherefore let them that suffer according to the will of God commit the keeping of their souls to him in well doing, as unto a faithful Creator" (1 Peter 4:19).

Thank God, suffering is always the short period before final victory! "But the God of all grace, who hath called us unto his eternal glory by Christ Jesus, after that ye have suffered a while, make you perfect, stablish, strengthen, settle you" (1 Peter 5:10).

6

Victory Over Your Besetting Sin

Sin causes Christians to become craven cowards who live in humiliating defeat. They can't stand up, with courage, against sin, because of the secret sin in their own lives. They excuse the sins of others, because of the disobedience in their own hearts; and they can't preach victory, because they live in defeat. Some of them once knew what it was like to live victoriously, taking vengeance against sin, having fulfilled Christ's righteousness in their own lives. They experienced the power, the courage, and the blessings, that come to those who are obedient to the Lord. Today they are but a shadow of their former selves. They hang their heads in shame, unable to look the world in the eye, victimized by a sin that rules their lives. A besetting sin has robbed them of their spiritual vitality, and one enemy after another is raised up against them.

A once mightily used evangelist now sells cars in a small town in Texas. He stood in the pulpit as a powerful preacher of the Gospel, and thousands were converted through his ministry. He became an adulterer, left his wife, and ran off with his girl friend. In just a few weeks, he lost everything. That minister is now but a shell of his old self. To see him shuffle about, beaten down and sad eyed, is pitiful. He lives in constant fear and spends sleepless nights thinking of what could have been. His anxieties have made him physically ill; he has chest pains, ulcers, and hypertension. He has repented of his sin, but he cannot undo the past. God forgives, but people don't!

A sixteen-year-old youth confessed to me: "I'm having sex with my girl friend. I've been reading what the Bible says about fornication and adultery, and now I'm scared. I worry that God will have to judge me, if the Bible is true. I keep doing it, and I'm full of fear, guilt, and worry. It seems as though there are two people inside of me, a good person and a bad person. I am afraid the bad person in me will overpower the good person, and God will have to give up on me. How can I make sure the good person in me gets the victory?"

Both the minister and the boy have been overpowered by their enemies of guilt, fear, and depression. They are victims, defeated and humiliated by unseen enemies that threaten to destroy them. Sin always brings on the enemies. Sin weakens all resistance; it turns warriors into weaklings. Lust conceives, then it brings on sin, and sin brings on the enemy to destroy.

We Must Learn From Examples in the Old Testament

David had enemies. They were the Philistines, the Amorites, the Ammonites, the Syrians, and other various enemies arrayed against Israel. When David was right with the Lord and in good fellowship, none of his enemies could stand before him. He slew them by the tens of thousands, and his name was feared in every enemy camp. But when David sinned and became estranged from the Lord, his enemies grew bold and triumphed over him. Sin caused him to lose his courage and confidence, making him weak before all his enemies.

David's sin of adultery immediately followed one of his greatest victories. The Ammonite-Syrian war was one of Israel's greatest battles. David gathered all Israel together, passed with them over Jordan, and did battle at Helam. The Syrians fled before Israel; seven hundred chariots were destroyed, forty thousand horsemen were killed, and all the kings allied to the Ammonites and Syrians fled. The chapter on this great war closes by saying, ". . . they made peace with Israel, and served them . . ." (2 Samuel 10:19).

This great man of God, basking in the glory of his greatest victory, began to lust after Bathsheba, killed her husband Uriah, and committed adultery with her. ". . . But the thing that David had done displeased the Lord" (2 Samuel 11:27).

So the Lord sent the Prophet Nathan to David. The prophet did not come with a message of love and understanding. He did not come to counsel David on how to handle his guilt and condemnation. He did not offer the king a salve for his stricken conscience. Rather, Nathan got right to the heart of the matter. "You are the man. You have despised the commandment of the Lord. You have done evil in the sight of the Lord. You are guilty of secret sin" (*see* 2 Samuel 12:7–9).

Sin Brings on Its Own Judgment

To a man after His own heart, God had to say, ". . . Behold, I will raise up evil against thee out of thine own house . . ." (2 Samuel 12:11). Shortly after, his beloved son Absalom turned against him, and David fled for his life into the wilderness. What a pitiful sight!

> And David went up by the ascent of mount Olivet, and wept as he went up, and had his head covered, and he went barefoot: and all the people that was with him covered every man his head, and they went up, weeping as they went up.
>
> 2 Samuel 15:30

Is this weeping, barefoot, broken man the same great king who, just months before, had defeated two world powers?

What turned him into a weak, powerless, cowardly man who fled before the enemy? It was sin—nothing else! Like Samson, David was shorn of his courage and power, because he caved in to the weakness of his flesh.

Solomon, too, was feared by all his enemies. Pharaoh's armies were held off by his powerful reputation. The Edomites dared not attack so powerful a king. His was a glorious reign, and his fame was unparalleled. He was blessed, prospered, and honored in everything he did. But Solomon sinned against the Lord and permitted his love for God to grow cold. He lost touch with heaven. And look what happened. God said to him, "Because you failed to keep my covenant and my statutes and have turned aside to other gods, I will rend the kingdom from you" (*see* 1 Kings 11:9–11).

Suddenly the enemies of Solomon fell upon him. "And the Lord stirred up an adversary unto Solomon, Hadad the Edomite . . ." (1 Kings 11:14). Not just one enemy, but two: "And God stirred him up another adversary, Rezon . . . and he abhorred Israel . . ." (1 Kings 11:23, 25).

Sin and compromise so weakened this mighty king that even his servant became an enemy. "And Jeroboam . . . Solomon's servant . . . even he lifted up his hand against the king" (1 Kings 11:26).

Not a single enemy of Israel could stand before her when that nation did what was right before God. Israel's enemies fled in terror at the mention of her name. The enemies' hearts melted like wax when the victorious armies of Israel went to war, with banners waving. But when Israel sinned, even her weakest enemies prevailed against her. Achan committed an accursed sin, and the minuscule army of Ai sent Israel running in humiliation and defeat.

Listen to the prayer of Solomon at the dedication of the temple, and you soon discover all Israel was very much aware of what made the nation victorious and what brought defeat upon the people:

When thy people Israel be smitten down before the
enemy, because they have sinned against thee. . . . If
they sin against thee, (for there is no man that sinneth
not,) and thou be angry with them, and deliver them to
the enemy. . . .

1 Kings 8:33,46

All the people of Israel had to do to maintain the copious
blessings of the Lord was harken diligently to the Lord's
commandments, love the Lord, and serve Him with all their
hearts and souls. God promised blessings beyond anything
they could imagine. God promised them:

There shall no man be able to stand before you: for the
Lord your God shall lay the fear of you and the dread of
you upon all the land that ye shall tread upon. . . .

Deuteronomy 11:25

Israel was told, "Behold, I set before you this day a blessing
and a curse; A blessing, if ye obey. . . . And a curse, if ye . . .
turn aside out of the way . . ." (Deuteronomy 11:26–28).

Is This Generation Bringing a Curse on Itself?

Such a very clear manifestation of God at work must not be
lost on us today. Is this why we are falling, as victims, before
our modern enemies? We do not fight against flesh and blood
enemies; ours are more powerful! Our enemies are fear, depression, guilt, condemnation, worry, anxiety, loneliness,
emptiness, despair.

Has God changed in His character, or does He still stir up
adversaries against a sinning, compromising generation? Can
it be that these modern-day enemies are overpowering many
of God's people because of their hidden sins and backsliding?

It was not a heavy yoke God put on His people. It was so
simple and easy: Obey and be blessed, or disobey and suffer!

That same message is echoed in the New Testament: "For to be carnally minded is death; but to be spiritually minded is life and peace" (Romans 8:6).

We have had quite enough teaching on how to cope with our problems and fears. We have not had enough teaching on how to deal with sin in our lives. You can't heal cancer by putting patches on it. It has to be removed. We will continue to be a neurosis-bound people as long as we excuse the sin in us. No wonder we are so depressed, worried, and burdened with guilt and condemnation; we continue to live in our disobedience and compromise.

Most of us are fully aware sin is at the root of all our problems. We know sin causes fear, guilt, and depression. We know it robs us of all spiritual courage and vitality. But what we do not know is how to overcome the sin that so easily besets us.

Most of the books I've read about achieving Christ's righteousness and living a holy life never tell me how to get and keep the victory over sin. We hear it preached at us all the time: "Sin is your enemy. God hates your sin. Walk in the Spirit. Forsake your evil ways. Lay aside that sin you keep indulging in. Don't be bound by the cords of your own iniquity." That's all well and good.

You Can't Just Walk Away From Your Besetting Sin

How do you overcome a sin that has become a habit? Where is the victory over a besetting sin that almost becomes a part of your life? You can hate that sin; you can keep swearing you will never do it again; you can cry and weep over it; you can live in remorse over what it does to you; but how do you walk away from it? How do you reach the point where that sin no longer enslaves you?

Recently I asked over three hundred seekers a very pointed question: "How many of you are fighting a losing battle against a besetting sin? How many have one secret sin that keeps dragging you down?" I was shocked at the quick reaction. Almost all of them admitted they were victims, seeking desperately to be delivered from sins that bound them.

Everywhere I go, I hear such horrible admissions of defeat and failure concerning this matter of victory over a besetting sin. Most are dedicated Christians who deeply love the Lord. They are not wicked or vile people; it's just that they have to admit, "I have this *one* problem that keeps me from being totally free."

The confessions are honest and heartrending:

- I can't tell anybody what my secret battle is; it's between the Lord and me. I've prayed for deliverance for over three years now. I've made a thousand promises to quit. I've lived in torment. The fear of God haunts me. I know it's wrong. But, try as I may, I keep doing it. I sometimes think I'm hooked forever. Why doesn't the Lord come down and take this thing away?

- You tell me to lay aside my sin? Great! I've done that hundreds of times. But my sin won't let go of me. Just when I think I've gotten the victory—WHAM—it comes back again. I've cried a river of tears over my sinfulness, and I'm tired of promising God I'll never do it again. All I want is to be free, but I don't know how. I know I'll never be what God wants me to be until I get the victory.

- I've been preaching to others for over fifteen years, but recently I fell into Satan's trap. I've been crippled spiritually, and, as much as I hate my besetting sin, I can't seem to get free of this bondage. None of the formulas and solutions I preached to others seem to work for me. Frankly, I wonder how long God will put up with me before I'm exposed.

Is There Victory Over All Our Habitual Sins?

I have no formulas, no simple solutions. I do know there is much comfort in the Bible for those who are fighting battles between the flesh and the spirit. Paul fought the same kinds of battles, against the same kinds of enemies. He confessed, "For the good that I would I do not: but the evil which I would not, that I do" (Romans 7:19).

Paul cried out, just as all mankind does, "O wretched man that I am! who shall deliver me from the body of this death?" (Romans 7:24). He goes on to say, "I thank God through Jesus Christ our Lord . . ." (Romans 7:25).

Yes, we know. Victory over all our enemies is through Jesus Christ the Lord. But how do we get the power out of His vine into our puny little branches? How does this thing work? I love Jesus—always have. I know He has all power. I know He promises me victory, but just what does it mean? How does the victory come? It's not enough to be forgiven; I must be free from going back to my sin.

I am just beginning to see a little light on this great mystery of godliness. God is asking me to do the following three things in my own search for total victory over all my besetting sins:

1.   I must learn to hunger for holiness and to hate my beset-
ting sin.   Every waking moment I must remind myself God hates my sin, mostly because of what it does to me. God hates it because it weakens me and makes me a coward; then I cannot be a vessel of honor to do His work on earth. If I excuse my sin as a weakness, if I make myself believe I am an exception and God will bend over backwards to comply with my needs, if I put out of mind all thoughts of divine retribution, then I am on the way to accepting my sin and opening myself to a reprobate mind. God wants me to loathe my sin, to hate it with all that is within me. There can be no victory or deliverance from sin until I am convinced God will not permit it!

The knowledge of God's retribution against sin is the basis of all freedom. God cannot look upon sin; He cannot condone it; He cannot make a single exception—so face it! It is wrong! Don't expect to be excused or to be given special privileges. God must act against all sin that threatens to destroy one of His children. It is wrong, and nothing will ever make it right! Sin pollutes the pure stream of holiness flowing through me. It must be confessed and forsaken. I must be convinced of that.

2. *I must be convinced God loves me in spite of my sin.* God hates my sin with a perfect hatred, while at the same time, He loves me with an infinite compassion. His love will never once compromise with sin, but He clings to His sinning child with one purpose in mind: to reclaim him.

His wrath against my sin is balanced by His great pity for me as His child. The moment He sees me hating my sin as He does, His pity conquers His loathing against sin. My motive must never be fear of God's wrath against my sin, but a willingness to accept His love that seeks to save me. If His love for me cannot save me, His wrath never will. It should be more than my sin that shames me and humbles me; it should be the knowledge that He keeps loving me in spite of all I've done to grieve Him.

Think of it! God pities me! He knows the agony of my battle. He is never far off; He is always there with me, reassuring me that nothing can ever separate me from His love. He knows my battle is enough burden, without forcing me to carry on with the added fear of wrath and judgment. I know His love for me will cause Him to withhold the rod while the battle is being fought. God will never hurt me, strike me, or abandon me while I am in the process of hating my sin and seeking help and deliverance. While I am swimming against the tide, He is always on shore, ready to throw me a lifeline.

3. *I must accept my Father's loving help in resisting and*

overcoming.   Sin is like an octopus with many tentacles trying to crush out my life. Seldom do all tentacles loosen their hold on me at once. It is one tentacle at a time. In this war against sin, it is a victory won through one soldier dying at a time. Seldom does the entire enemy army fall dead at a single blast. It is hand-to-hand combat. It is one small victory at a time. But God doesn't send me out to do battle without a war plan. He is my Commander; I will fight—inch by inch, hour by hour—under His direction.

He dispatches the Holy Spirit to me, with clear directions on how to fight, when to run, where to strike next. This battle against principalities and powers is His war against the devil, not mine. I am just a soldier, fighting in His war. I may get weary, wounded, and discouraged, but I can keep on fighting when I know He must give me the orders. I am a volunteer in His war. I am ready to do His will at all costs. I will wait for His orders on how to win. Those directions come slowly at times. The battle seems to go against me, but in the end, I know we win. God wants me to just believe in Him. Like Abraham, my faith is counted to me as righteousness. The only part I can play in this war is to believe God will bring me, victorious, out of the battle.

Finally, When the Sin in Me Is Conquered, All My Other Enemies Must Flee

What I do about the sin in my life determines how my enemies will behave. Victory over besetting sin causes all my other enemies to flee. Worry, fear, guilt, anxiety, depression, restlessness, and loneliness are all my enemies. But they can harm me only when sin turns me into an unprotected target. The righteous are as bold as lions. They have clear minds and consciences, and those are fortresses these enemies cannot overrun.

Do you want victory over all your enemies? Then go at it the right way, by dealing ferociously with your besetting sin. Remove the accursed thing in your life, and you will become mighty in God. ". . . let us lay aside every weight, and the sin which doth so easily beset [surround or harass] us . . ." (Hebrews 12:1).

7

How to Win Over Temptation

Temptation is an invitation or an enticement to commit an immoral act. And right now Satan is raging over the earth, as a roaring lion, trying to devour Christians through powerful enticements toward immorality. No one is immune, and the closer you get to God, the more Satan will desire to sift you.

Sinners cannot be tempted; only true children of God can be. Rain cannot touch a body already under water. Sinners are already drowned in perdition. As children of Satan, they do as he dictates. They do not have to be tempted or enticed, because they are already immoral, already condemned. As slaves, they are not free to choose. They simply go from dead to twice dead to being plucked up by the roots. Sinners can be teased by the devil, but not tempted. Satan teases his own children into deeper and darker pits of immorality. They are already dead in their trespasses and sins and no longer fight the battles of the living. That's why our Lord tells us to rejoice when we fall into divers temptations. We are experiencing something unique only to maturing Christians.

Temptation is training under combat conditions. It is limited warfare. God limits that warfare to the point of being bearable. God wants combat-seasoned warriors who can testify, "I was under fire! I've been in the battle! The enemy was all around me, shooting at me, trying to kill me, but God showed me how to take it and not be afraid. I have experience now, so the next time I'll not fear."

Temptation is not a sign of weakness or a leaning toward the world. Rather, it is a graduation, a sign God trusts us. The Spirit led Jesus into the arena of temptation in the wilderness so He could learn the secret of power over all temptation. Actually God was saying to Jesus, "Son, I have given You the Spirit without measure. I have confirmed You before the world. Now I am going to permit Satan to throw at You every device he has, to tempt You with his most potent enticements. I will do this so You will never once fear his dominion, so You may go forth, preaching the kingdom, with faith that Satan is defeated; and You will know he cannot touch You in any way."

That is why Christians are tempted today—not to teach us something about ourselves, not to show off the power of the devil. No! Temptation is allowed in the saintliest of lives to teach us the limitation of Satan, to defang the devil, to expose his weakness, to reveal Satan as a scarecrow. We fear only what we do not understand.

Satan is just like the Wizard of Oz, who uses all kinds of scary devices to frighten unenlightened people. What a horror show he puts on: a tinseled display of power, strength, and dominion. But God knows it is all feeble noise and phoniness. Behind the stage is a weak wizard: the insignificant, powerless, bespectacled little bald-headed creature pushing buttons and pulling levers. Who in his right mind, knowing the mighty power of God, could but laugh at Satan's puny sideshow?

When we are tempted, it is God's way of saying to us, "Satan is powerless; he is not what he claims to be. He wears a false mask and shoots out fiery darts that fizzle and die in the presence of truth. But you must discover this yourself. Go into his circus. Stand up to his cheap threats, then conquer your fear of him. He will not scare you; he will not expose weakness in you. He cannot make you do anything. Instead, you will discover his weakness. You will expose him as a phony wizard. Then he will flee from you, because he doesn't want you to share with anyone else the secret you have learned."

It is not enough to say it is no sin to be tempted. That means absolutely nothing to those who have already yielded. The problem is not in learning how to accept temptation as an experience all Christians go through, but rather what to do to avoid giving in. The problem is how to bear up when Satan snares us in his trap! We want to know how to get the power and courage to say no and stick with it, how to find power to plan not to give in. When Satan comes in on us like a flood, there is no time to run to a secret closet for help. There may not be time to grab a Bible and seek out a few powerful promises to encourage us. There may not be a strong Christian friend around to hold us up in prayer. Suddenly temptation is upon us, and immediate decisions must be made. That makes it all the more important that Christians carry with them, at all times, the secret of bearing up anytime, anywhere, under any and all temptations.

Power to bear up and not yield to temptation does not come from stuffing our minds with Scripture verses, in making vows and promises, in spending hours in prayer and fasting, in surrounding ourselves with godly Christian friends and influences, or in giving ourselves over to a great spiritual cause. These things are all commendable and normal for Christian growth, but that is not where our victory lies.

Break the Fear of Satan's Power

The simple secret of bearing up under any temptation is to break the fear of Satan's power. Fear is the only power Satan has over man. God does not give us the spirit of fear; that is of Satan only. But man is afraid of the devil, demons, failure; that his appetites and habits can't be altered; that inner desires will erupt and control his life. He is afraid he is one of a thousand who may be different: innately weak, full of lust, and beyond help.

Man is afraid he can't quit his sin. He credits Satan with power he doesn't have. Man cries out, "I'm hooked! I can't stop. I'm spellbound and in the devil's power. The devil makes me do it!"

Fear has torment! As long as you are afraid of the devil, you can never break the power of any temptation. That is why Satan is promoting films like *The Exorcist, The Omen,* and a barrage of movies that make people vomit and faint in fear; that is why Satan is delighted with the teaching, now creeping into some churches, that demons can possess Christians. Satan thrives on fear, and Christians who are afraid of the devil have little or no power to resist his enticements.

It's all based on a lie! That lie is that Satan has power to break down Christians under pressure. Not so! Jesus came to destroy all the power of the devil over blood-washed children of God. I often wondered why God allowed spiritual people to be so tempted. Why doesn't God remove all temptation instead of "making a way of escape that we may be able to bear it"? (*See* 1 Corinthians 10:13.) The answer is simple: Once we learn how powerless Satan is, once we learn he can't make us do anything, once we learn God has all power to keep us from falling—then we can bear up under anything Satan throws at us. We can go through it without fearing we will fall!

The Move You Make Right After You Fail

You have heard it said it is not a sin to be tempted. I say it is not the greatest sin to give in to temptation. The greatest of all sins is not believing God has power to deliver us and keep us from yielding again! As a Christian, the most important move you will ever make is the move you make right after you fail!

We are not delivered from temptation, but from the fear of the devil to make us yield to it. We will keep on being tempted until we come to the place of rest in our faith. That rest is an unshakable confidence God has defeated Satan; Satan has no right or claim on us; and we will come forth as gold tried in the fire.

A double-minded person is unstable in all his ways. He is a person who believes the power is equally divided between God and Satan, which explains why some ". . . in time of temptation fall away" (Luke 8:13). They fall back into fear; they lose sight of God's mighty power; they cower under Satan's fear mongering. Jesus taught us to pray we not be led into temptation. We are to watch and pray that we "enter not into temptation." The spirit is willing, but the flesh is weak. The Spirit of God in us yearns to teach us confidence in God's power, but the flesh seeks to give in to fear.

I believe it was fear, not weariness, that put the disciples to sleep while Jesus prayed in the Garden. They had just received the news of His betrayal, that Jesus would be delivered into the hands of sinful men, that Peter would become a traitor, that they would all be offended and scattered. Suddenly they forgot all His miracles, His mighty power to heal the sick and raise the dead, His power to multiply loaves and fishes. They were now terrified. They feared for their flesh. They feared being abandoned by the Lord. They slept the sleep of doomed men.

When Jesus asks us to pray that we won't be led into temptation, He is actually saying, "Pray you learn to trust God's power now, instead of having to go back again and again into the arena of temptation, until the lesson is learned!" Pray you will not have to be led into temptation, because the lesson you would be taught has already been learned.

We Overcome by Faith Alone

The Bible says God knows ". . . how to deliver the godly out of temptations . . ." (2 Peter 2:9). How? By putting us under fire, until we come out singing, "Greater is he that is in me than he that is in the world" (*see* 1 John 4:4), until we learn we overcome by faith alone, until we acknowledge once and for all, ". . . For this purpose the Son of God was manifested, that he might destroy the works of the devil" (1 John 3:8).

You don't *have* to yield to temptation, but at times you may. Even the saintliest of God's people occasionally do. That is why God made special provisions for those who fail: ". . . if any man sin, we have an advocate with the Father, Jesus Christ the righteous" (1 John 2:1).

Our Lord is not nearly as grieved by our yielding to temptation as He is by our not learning how to deal with it. He is more hurt by the fact that we have not trusted His power to deliver. God is hurt, not so much by what we do, as He is by what we do not do. Jesus wept over the city of Jerusalem, deeply grieved; not because of the sin in that city; not because of the alcoholism, prostitution, adultery, lying, and cheating; but because He offered peace and deliverance, and they would not accept! They would not come in simple faith. They would not take Him at His word. They would not run to the shelter of His protecting wing. Their unbelief in His power made Him weep. A sinner is one who lives as one who confesses the devil has more power than God. The overcoming Christian is one whose life confesses, "God has the kingdom, the power, and the glory forever! Amen."

Some people really don't want to be free from their temptation. They flirt and play with it as a kind of spiritual brinkmanship. They know God can keep them from their sin, but deep inside they prefer to have a season of fun, a few rounds of immorality, a little taste of the forbidden. They are afraid to trust God for power to overcome, because they are not really sure they want out. It is too enticing! They don't want to grieve the Lord or turn their backs on His love. They want to be delivered—after a while. They want a halfway deliverance, just in time. Too many today are afraid to turn it all over to the Lord, because they still hunger after Satan's alluring enticement. Satan always makes yielding so convenient, so simple, so easy.

God Gives Us a Will to Overcome

God has the power to make us want to be free. He can put in us a will to overcome and the power to perform that will. If Satan can put a will in man to sin, God can and does put in His children the will to overcome. Our part is to simply believe God can sanctify our will and put in us an overpowering desire to resist the devil's invitation: "For it is God which worketh in you both to will and to do of his good pleasure" (Philippians 2:13).

Do you want power to bear up under all temptation? Do you want a way of escape? Do you want a growing strength to resist? Then quit glorifying the devil! Stop thinking he can force you to sin! He has no power to addict you to anything! Use your shield of faith! Look right into the eye of that storm of temptation, and cry out, ". . . that wicked one toucheth me not" (*see* 1 John 5:18). Conquer your fear of the devil's power, and you can forever after bear any temptation he sends your way. Simply commit the keeping of your faith unto Him, as a faithful Creator.

Most important of all remember this: ". . . stand fast. . . . And in nothing terrified by your adversaries . . ." (*see* Philippians 1:27, 28).

8

Christian, Lay Down Your Guilt

Christians are strange creatures. They travel the world, preaching the love of Jesus and His forgiveness for any and all sin. They tell the heathen, the addict, the alcoholic, the prostitute: "Come to Christ and be forgiven. He forgave your sins at the cross, so come and receive forgiveness and healing for all your hurts. You can have peace and be free of guilt." As a result, sinners who have been guilty of every conceivable kind of dark and evil deed gladly come to Christ and are instantly forgiven and delivered from their guilt.

The hardest thing in the world for the Christian to do is receive for himself the same kind of love and forgiveness he preaches to sinners. We Christians find it so very difficult to allow ourselves the same freedom from guilt we offer, through Christ, to harlots and drunkards.

Christians sin against the Lord, then proceed to carry about an excruciating load of guilt. They want to pay for their failure. They want to be punished. They want to do penance or suffer some kind of hurt before they are forgiven.

"But Lord," argues the Christian, "I sinned with my eyes wide open; I knew better. I knew before I did it I was breaking a commandment. How can I be forgiven for grieving my

Saviour by such insolence? I shook off the conviction of the Holy Spirit and stubbornly went ahead and committed sin."

The Danger of Guilt

Guilt is dangerous in that it destroys faith. The enemy of our souls is not at all interested in making Christians into adulterers, addicts, or prostitutes. He is interested in one thing only, and that is turning Christians into unbelievers. He uses the lusts of the body to bind the mind.

Satan did not want Job to become an adulterer or an addict to pain pills or a wine guzzler. No! Satan wanted one thing of Job: He wanted him to curse God! He wanted to destroy Job's faith in God.

So it is today. Our real battle is not really with sex, alcohol, drugs, or lust. It is with our faith. Do we believe God is a deliverer? Is He there to help in the hour of temptation? Are His promises true? Is there freedom from sin? Is God really answering prayer today? Will He bring us out of the battle, victorious? Will joy follow weeping?

Satan wants you to be so crushed with guilt that you let go of your faith. He wants you to doubt God's faithfulness. He wants you to think nobody really cares, that you will live in misery and heartbreak, that you will always be a slave to your lust, that God's holiness is unreachable, that you are left alone to work out your own problems, that God no longer cares about your needs and feelings. If he can get you to the point of despair, he can flood you with unbelief. Then he has succeeded in his mission. The three simple steps toward atheism are guilt, doubt, and unbelief.

Guilt, like a raging cancer, can eat away at the spiritual vitality of a Christian. It causes a person to lose control of life; it leads to a desire to quit or retire from spiritual activity; and it finally brings on physical pain and disease. Like cancer,

guilt feeds upon itself, until all spiritual life is gone. Weakness
and a sense of shame and failure are the end results.

I meet Christians across this nation who go about continually burdened down by an overwhelming load of guilt. They
have made themselves believe they are traitors to the Lord.
They live in spiritual agony and grief every waking hour,
because of some hidden sin or weakness. They cannot appro-
priate divine forgiveness for themselves, and they live in
dreaded fear of God's judgment upon themselves or their
families.

The Causes of Guilt

Who are these guilt-ridden, sad souls? It is often that married individual who, for years, has been a captive in a loveless
marriage and finds someone else to light up his boring life.
Somewhere along the way, that marriage lost its romance.
Hurts would no longer heal; the lines of communication were
cut. Then one day, without even seeking it, someone else
enters the picture. A tender word, a tender touch, and there
is a new kind of awakening. Someone else ignites those dying
embers, and the secret love affair is born. They take comfort
in the words of the song that says, "How can it be wrong,
when it seems so right?"

Often there are children to consider, a reputation, a job, or
a ministry. But the one thing above all else that brings on the
guilt is the knowledge that God's laws are being broken. God
won't smile on it; He won't put His blessing on it. Then the
war begins. They are torn between a conviction of having
finally found the one true love of life and the innate desire to
stay true to God and marriage vows. And the guilt keeps
piling up. They want out of a hopeless marriage, without
displeasing God.

There are multiplied thousands caught in this kind of trap,

even ministers. The more they love God, the worse their guilt. A few are able to shake off the guilt and go about indulging their secret affairs, having justified their actions with elaborate excuses. But most cannot be dishonest with their own hearts, so they go on living with accumulating guilt.

What about all those other secret lusts of the flesh which haunt the soul? What about the Christian who overindulges in drink on the sly or who has too many prescription drugs which have caused a dependency? What about the thousands of Christian men caught up in porno binges? A strange attraction sends them back into the X-rated movie houses or to the newsstands for nudie magazines—not once or twice, but nearly every time they are alone, especially when traveling. Yes, I'm talking about Christians.

Secret affairs, drinking, prescription drugs, pornography, homosexuality, lesbianism, and many other human weaknesses are all prime causes of guilt. The sinner can indulge in any or all of these sins and not battle with guilt, but not so for the true child of God.

Saints That Ain't

Sadly, many pious Christians hide behind puritan masks and go about like the publican of Christ's time, who boasted, "Thank God I'm not like such sinners." To hear them tell it, their marriages are flawless and their morals are saintlike. Don't believe it! We have all sinned and come short of God's holiness. There are none righteous in their own strength. Show me the saintliest soul on earth, and I'll show you one who battles temptation as much as any other Christian alive. And if a Christian would like to cure himself of being judgmental, all he has to do is look inside himself and be honest about his own inner struggles. That should keep us all from worrying about another's spiritual condition.

One of the good things that should come out of a Christian's inner struggle with the flesh is that he learns to quit throwing stones—that is, if he is honest with himself. The Word instructs, ". . . even as Christ forgave you, so also do ye" (Colossians 3:13).

Perhaps out of all the terrible struggles Christians are now enduring, we will discover a new spirit of tolerance and love for others. Perhaps, being forgiven so much ourselves, we will in turn forgive others, for their shortcomings: ". . . be ye kind one to another, tenderhearted, forgiving one another, even as God for Christ's sake hath forgiven you" (Ephesians 4:32).

Tested by the Word

Is there freedom from guilt? Can Christians deal with infatuations, addictions, and weaknesses in an honest and godly way and find true freedom from sin's power? Will God keep forgiving while the struggle goes on? If that besetting sin keeps overcoming the believer, will God continue to forgive until the victory comes?

There have been some very godly people who have confessed to me that God's Word tried them severely. The promises sound as if they should work almost automatically, but they don't. The commandment says don't, but our weak flesh can't seem to obey. We go ahead and do what we know to be sinful. The Word says, ". . . sin hath no more dominion over you" (*see* Romans 6:9). Yet it doesn't seem to work in everyday life.

> O wretched man that I am! who shall deliver me from
> the body of this death? I thank God through Jesus Christ
> our Lord. So then with the mind I myself serve the law
> of God; but with the flesh the law of sin.
>
> Romans 7:24, 25

The question is: Where do I get the power to resist the lust of my heart? Is it sheer willpower? Do I grit my teeth and say, "I'll simply walk away from it, never to let it hold me in its power"? Does God expect me to resist with what I have? Can I win over my besetting sin, in one moment of finality?

Others say glibly, "Just stop it! Quit it! Walk away from it! You know better, so what's so difficult?" Oh, yes! But those same people who find it so easy to walk away from all the lusts of the flesh and the desires of the world find it nearly impossible to walk away from their own loneliness, sorrows, fears, or struggles with health. Every Christian on this earth fights inner battles; not one is immune!

The way to get rid of guilt is to get rid of sin. It sounds simple, but it isn't. You don't just make up your mind to drop the third party who has entered your life. Many have tried that and found it didn't work. You don't just walk away from things that bind. The Scripture haunts you; it says, "Put off the old man. . . . Lay aside the besetting sin. . . . Flee the appearance of evil. . . . Walk in the Spirit and you will not fulfill the lusts of the flesh." That is exactly what you want: freedom from the sin that so easily besets you, to walk in the Spirit completely, and to live a life totally pleasing to God. But you seem helpless in putting off those desires.

When you can't seem to overcome, and you keep falling flat on your face, failure after failure, then you begin to think, "Something is terribly wrong with me. I am a sensuous, wicked, weak child. God must be fed up with all my failures. I've made Him mad." That is when guilt floods in like a tidal wave.

We All Face the Same Struggles

Take heart, child of God. Everybody is in the same boat. Not all of us battle a secret affair or an addiction to the flesh. Some of us struggle with a more insidious enemy: doubt. To doubt God's concern and daily involvement in our lives can cause terrible guilt. But there is no temptation befallen you that is not common to all men. You are not going through some strange trial, unique only to you. Thousands more are going through the very same struggle.

The most important move you will ever make in your life is the move you make right after you fail God. Will you believe the accuser's lies and give up in despair, or will you allow yourself to receive the forgiving flow of God's love, which you preach so much to others?

Do you fear asking His forgiveness because you are not really sure you want to be free from that thing which holds you? Do you want the Lord, yet secretly long for something or someone not lawfully yours? God is able, in answer to sincere prayer, to make you want to do His perfect will. Ask Him to make you want to fulfill His will. "For it is God which worketh in you both to will and to do of his good pleasure" (Philippians 2:13).

When a Christian sins, he feels shut out of God's presence, just as Adam did. God is always there, waiting to talk, but sin causes man to withdraw. God never withdraws; only man withdraws. Actually the person living in sin is afraid to open up to God, for fear He will ask a commitment to holiness before the sin is ready to be surrendered. The sinning Christian knows this: "If I get close to Jesus, the Holy Spirit will put His finger on my secret sin, and I'll have to give it up. I'm not ready for that yet!"

It does no good to ask yourself, "How did I get into this mess? Why do I have to be tempted along these lines? Why such a trial, when I didn't ask for it or want it? Why me, Lord?" Don't blame the devil either. We sin when we are drawn away and enticed by the lust of our own hearts.

Don't Justify Your Weaknesses

Never justify your wrongdoing. There is only one way to become hardened by sin, and that is to justify it. Christians who learn to hate their sin will never give themselves over to its power. As Christians, we must never lose sight of the exceeding sinfulness of sin. Stay uncomfortable with your sin.

I heard it said of an evangelist who lives in open, shameless adultery, "Well, at least he is honest about it. He's not trying to hide his adultery, as some ministers, who do it on the sly." I see nothing honest in that at all! That adulterous evangelist has been totally blinded by a multiplicity of justifications. He has no guilt, because he has given himself over to a lie and has become the victim of a reprobate mind. On the other hand, the person who continues to struggle, hating a garment spotted, despising all sin against God, has all heaven standing by to help. Until the victory comes, continue to despise all your wrongdoing.

Never Limit God's Forgiveness

My dear Christian friend, never limit God's forgiveness to you. His forgiveness and longsuffering have no limit. Jesus told His disciples: "And if he trespass against thee seven times in a day, and seven times in a day turn again to thee, saying, I repent; thou shalt forgive him" (Luke 17:4).

Can you believe such a thing? Seven times a day this person willfully sins before my very eyes, then says, "I'm sorry." And I am to forgive him, continuously. How much more will our heavenly Father forgive His children who come in repentance to Him? Don't stop to reason it out. Don't ask how or why He forgives so freely. Simply accept it.

Jesus did not say, "Forgive your brother once or twice, then tell him to go and sin no more. Tell him if he ever does it again, he will be cut off. Tell him he is a habitual, hopeless sinner." No! Jesus called for unlimited, no-strings-attached forgiveness!

It is God's nature to forgive. David said, "For thou, Lord,

art good, and ready to forgive; and plenteous in mercy unto all them that call upon thee" (Psalms 86:5).

God is waiting, right now, to flood your being with the joy of forgiveness. You need only to open up all the doors and windows of your soul and allow His Spirit to flood you with forgiveness.

John, speaking as a Christian, wrote: "And he is the propitiation for our sins: and not for our's only, but also for the sins of the whole world" (1 John 2:2).

According to John, the goal of every Christian is to sin not. That means the Christian is not bent toward sin but, instead, leans toward God. But what happens when that God-leaning child sins?

> . . . And if any man sin, we have an advocate with the Father, Jesus Christ the righteous: If we confess our sins, he is faithful and just to forgive us our sins, and to cleanse us from all unrighteousness.
>
> 1 John 2:1, 1:9

Lay Down Your Guilt, Now

You don't just lay down your guilt, your sin, or your inner struggle as if it were a jacket you strip from your back. You lay it all down through a supernatural operation of God's Holy Spirit. The Holy Spirit responds to the broken heart that reaches out, in faith, to lay hold of God's promises. He then imparts His divine nature to that empty vessel. A miraculous series of events begins to unfold. Suddenly there comes to the saint of God a renewed desire to confess, to yield to God's will, to become more like Jesus, to see things in the light of eternity, to experience a rush of surrender.

The Holy Spirit brings the yielded vessel around to God's way of thinking. We go after things we believe are good for us; we covet what is not ours. But God looks way down the road, and He knows what is best. Our ways and thoughts are not His ways or His thoughts. God will give His surrendered child something even better, if he lays down his own plan.

What is it that stands between you and God? Is it a secret sin? Lust? Doubt? Fear? Anxiety? What is the cause of your guilt? Be willing to lay it down in surrender at the foot of the cross. Have a funeral right there; do your hurting and dying; then rise up in obedience, and walk in the Spirit. God will not let you down. He will replace that empty place with something far better, something pleasing to His own heart, something providing more joy to you than what you gave up.

Lay down your guilt, my friend. You don't need to carry that load another minute. Open up all the doors and windows of your heart, and let God's love in. He forgives you over and over again. He will give you the power to see your struggle through to victory. If you ask, if you repent—you are forgiven! Accept it now.

9

Stop Condemning Yourself

I feel so ashamed of myself when I think back over my early ministry, because I condemned so many sincere people. I meant well, and often my zeal was honest and well-meaning. But how many people I brought under terrible condemnation because they didn't conform to my ideas of holiness!

Years ago I preached against makeup on ladies. I preached against short dresses. I condemned everything that was not on my "legitimate" list. I have preached some very powerful sermons in the past, condemning homosexuals, divorcées, drinkers, and compromisers. I am still deeply committed to the idea that ministers must cry out against the inroads of sin and compromise in the lives of Christians. I still don't like to see Christian women painted up like streetwalkers. I still don't like mini-dresses. I believe, more than ever, that God hates divorce. I am still committed to the idea that God will not wink at any sin or compromise of any kind.

But lately God has been urging me to quit condemning people who have failed and, instead, preach to them a message of love and reconciliation. Why? Because the church today is filled with Christians who are burdened down with mountains of guilt and condemnation. They don't need more preaching about judgment and fear; they are already filled with enough fear and anxiety. They don't need to hear a preacher tell them how mad God is with them; they are already too much afraid of God's wrath. They need to hear the message John preached: "For God sent not his Son into the world to condemn the world; but that the world through him might be saved" (John 3:17).

Jesus said to an adulterous woman, ". . . Neither do I condemn thee; go, and sin no more!" (John 8:11). Now why can't I, and all my fellow ministers, preach that same kind of loving message to the multiplied thousands who live in fear and adultery? Why do we still condemn divorced Christians who remarry, when they have truly repented and have determined to sin no more in that manner?

Recently a ten-year-old lad stopped me after a crusade and begged me to hear his story. He was hysterical. "My mom and dad got divorced two years ago. Mom is a good Christian, and she married a nice Christian man. I live with mom and my stepdad, and I love them a whole lot. But my mom is always sad, and she cries a lot, because a minister told her she was living in sin. Is my mom going to hell because she got divorced and remarried another divorced man? I'm all confused, because they're both such good Christians."

I told that boy what I want to tell the whole world. If she divorced because of her own adultery and remarried, she is living in adultery. God hates adultery. But if she has repented, God forgives her, and she starts all over, like a newborn Christian. She is not living in sin when it is under the blood of Christ and forgiven. She can begin a new life without guilt or condemnation. If Jesus forgives murder, thievery, lying, and so on, He also forgives adultery.

It amazes me that we ministers are so willing to go to Africa to preach forgiveness to the heathen, but so unwilling to preach forgiveness and reconciliation to Christians at home. One minister complained to me about all the divorced, broken, troubled people in his new assignment. I thought, *My brother, you ought to be thankful God put you in such a fertile field. Those are the people who need your help the most. They need a man of God to show them how to begin anew.*

I am a happily married man; and, God helping me, Gwen and I will always be together, till death do us part. I despise divorce with a passion! But it troubles me that the church is willing to write off all those who have made a mistake. The church offers comfort and solace to all those who are the innocent victims—the wife who was cheated on, the husband whose wife walked out on him, all the children hurt in the separations.

But what about all the perpetrators—the sinners, the ones who wronged innocent loved ones? If one out of every three marriages ends in divorce, that means millions of husbands and wives are the guilty parties. I'm not willing to give up, even on the guilty ones. The thief Christ forgave at Calvary was not an innocent victim. No! He was a perpetrator; he was the criminal! But in his sin he turned to Christ in faith. He was forgiven and taken with Christ to glory.

What about homosexuals and lesbians and alcoholics? Will condemning them accomplish any good? No! A thousand times, no! Christ did not come to condemn these sinners, but to rescue them in love. God hates homosexual acts, but He does not despise people who do not live up to masculine or feminine roles.

A lovely nineteen-year-old nurse stopped me after a crusade. Tearfully, she sobbed out a pitiful confession: "Mr. Wilkerson, I'm a lesbian. I feel so dirty, so unclean. The minister of the church I used to attend asked me to never return. He said he couldn't take a chance on my seducing others in his congregation. I feel as if suicide is my only way out. I live in total fear and condemnation. Must I kill myself to find peace?"

She kept backing away from me, as if she were too unclean to be in my presence. I asked her if she still loved Jesus. "Oh, yes," she replied. "Every waking hour my heart cries out to Him. I love Christ with everything in me, but I'm bound by this terrible habit."

How beautiful it was to see her face light up when I told her how much God loved her, even in her struggles. I told her, "Don't ever give yourself over to your sin. God draws a line right where you are. Any momentum toward Him is accounted as righteousness. Any move back across that line, away from Him, is sin. If we draw near to Him, He draws near to us. Keep your spiritual momentum! Keep loving Jesus, even though you still do not have total victory. Accept His daily forgiveness. Live one day at a time. Be convinced that Jesus loves sinners, so He must love you, too!"

She smiled a smile of relief and said, "Mr. Wilkerson, you are the first minister who ever offered me a ray of hope. Deep in my heart I know He still loves me, and I know He will give me deliverance from this bondage. But I have been so condemned by everybody. Thanks for your message of hope and love."

Are you living under condemnation? Have you sinned against the Lord? Have you grieved the Holy Spirit in your life? Are you waging a losing battle with an overpowering temptation?

All you need to do is search God's Word, and you will discover a God of mercy, love, and endless compassion. David said: "If thou, Lord, shouldest mark iniquities, O Lord, who shall stand? But there is forgiveness with thee, that thou mayest be feared" (Psalms 130:3, 4).

A distraught woman who had come to my office sobbed, "Mr. Wilkerson, once God cured me of alcoholism. But recently I got discouraged and went back to drink. Now I can't stop. I've failed the Lord so badly that all I can do is give up. After all He did for me, look how I've failed Him. It's no use; I'll just never make it."

I'm convinced there are more spiritual failures than many of us realize. There is a demonic strategy to build such failures into walls to keep the defeated ones far from God. But we don't need to let the devil turn our temporary defeats into a permanent hell.

I believe there are literally millions of people like the young sailor who came to see me. With tears in his eyes he said, "My dad is a minister, but I've failed him so terribly. I'm so weak. I'm afraid I'll never serve the Lord as I should. I'm so easily led into sin."

Confessions such as these are tragic, but I have found great encouragement in the realization that some of the greatest men and women of the Bible had times of failure and defeat.

Would you consider Moses a failure? Hardly! He was to Israel what Washington and Lincoln, together, were to America—and much more. But look closely at the great lawgiver's life. His career began with a murder, followed by forty years of hiding from justice.

Moses was a man of fear and unbelief. When God called him to lead the Israelites out of slavery, he pleaded, ". . . I am not eloquent . . . I am slow of speech. . . . Send . . . by the hand of him whom thou wilt send" (Exodus 4:10, 13). This angered God. All his life, Moses longed to enter the Promised Land, but his failures kept him out. Even so, God compares Moses' faithfulness to Christ's. His failures did not keep Moses out of God's hall of champions: ". . . consider . . . Christ Jesus; Who was faithful to him that appointed him, as also Moses was faithful in all his house" (Hebrews 3:1, 2).

We usually think of Jacob as the great prayer warrior who
wrestled with the angel of the Lord and prevailed. Jacob was
given a vision of heaven with angels ascending and descend-
ing. Yet this man's life was filled with glaring failures, and
Scripture does not hide any of them.

As a youth, Jacob deceived his blind father, to steal his
brother's inheritance. Married, he despised his wife Leah,
while he nursed a great secret love for her sister, Rachel. He
did not accept his responsibility as a husband. After the birth
of each man-child, Leah kept saying, ". . . Now this time will
my husband be jointed unto me . . ." (Genesis 29:34). But
the fact was that Jacob hated her.

Here was a man caught in a web of trickery, graft, theft,
unfaithfulness, and polygamy. Nevertheless, we still worship
the God of Abraham, Isaac, and Jacob.

King David, singer of Psalms and mighty warrior, delighted
in the law of the Lord and posed as the righteous man who
would not stand among sinners. Yet how shocking are the
weaknesses of this great man. Taking Bathsheba from her
husband Uriah, he sent that unsuspecting man to his death, at
the front lines of his army. The Prophet Nathan declared that
this double sin gave great occasion for the enemies of the Lord
to blaspheme.

Picture the great king standing by the casket of his dead,
illegitimate child, a stolen wife at his side, and a world filled
with enemies who cursed God because of his notorious sins.
David stood there, a total failure. Yet God called David a man
after His own heart. He blessed the murderer Moses and the
schemer Jacob, too, because these men learned how to profit
from their failures and go on to victory.

If you are discouraged by your failures, I have good news
for you. No one is closer to the kingdom of God than the man
or woman or young person who can look defeat in the eye,
learn to face it, and move on to a life of peace and victory.

Don't Be Afraid of Failure

This seems like an automatic reaction. When Adam sinned, he tried to hide from God. When Peter denied Christ, he was afraid to face Him. When Jonah refused to preach to Nineveh, his fear drove him into the ocean, to flee the presence of the Lord.

But God has shown me a truth that has helped me many times: Something much worse than failure is the fear that goes with it. Adam, Jonah, and Peter ran away from God, not because they lost their love for Him, but because they were afraid He was too angry with them to understand. Satan uses such fear to make people think there is no use trying.

That old accuser of the brethren waits, like a vulture, for you to fail in some way. Then he uses every lie in hell to make you give up, to convince you God is too holy or you are too sinful to come back. Or he makes you afraid you are not perfect enough or that you will never rise above your failure.

It took forty years to get the fear out of Moses and to make him usable in God's program. Meanwhile God's plan of deliverance had to be delayed for nearly half a century while one man learned to face his failure. If Moses or Jacob or David had resigned himself to failure, we might never again have heard of these men. Yet Moses rose up again to become one of God's greatest heroes. Jacob faced his sins, was reunited with the brother he had cheated, and reached new heights of victory. David ran into the house of God, laid hold of the horns of the altar, found forgiveness and peace, and returned to his finest hour. Jonah retraced his steps, did what he had refused at first to do, and brought a whole city-state to repentance and deliverance. Peter rose out of the ashes of denial to lead a church to Pentecost.

Despite Failure, Keep Moving On

It is always after a failure that a man does his greatest work for God.

Twenty-one years ago, I sat in my little car, weeping; I was a terrible failure, I thought. I had been unceremoniously dumped from a courtroom after I thought I was led by God to witness to seven teenage murderers. I had seen my picture in the tabloids, over the caption, "Bible waving preacher interrupts murder trial." My attempt to obey God and to help those young hoodlums looked as though it were ending in horrible failure.

I shudder to think of how much blessing I would have missed if I had given up in that dark hour. How glad I am today that God taught me to face my failure and go on to His next step for me.

I know of two outstanding men of God, both of whom had ministered to thousands of people, who fell into the sin David committed with Bathsheba. One minister decided he could not go on. Today he drinks and curses the Christ he once preached about. The other man repented and started all over. He now heads an international missions program which reaches thousands for Christ. His failure has been left behind. He keeps moving forward.

In my work with narcotics addicts and incorrigibles, I have observed that the majority of those who return to their old habits become stronger than all the others when they face their failures and return to the Lord. They have a special awareness of the power of Satan, a total rejection of confidence in the flesh.

Despite Failure, Continue to Worship

There was only one way for Moses to stay in victory, because he had a disposition like so many of us today. He continually communed with the Lord, ". . . face to face, as a man speaketh unto his friend . . ." (Exodus 33:11). Moses maintained that close friendship with God. I believe the secret of holiness is very simple: Stay close to Jesus! Keep looking into His face, until you become like the image you behold.

One evening, a hysterical woman stopped me on the street and blurted out a terrible confession. Clutching my sleeve so hard I thought she would tear it, she said, "Mr. Wilkerson, I am facing the darkest hour of my life. I don't know which way to turn. My husband has left me, and it's all my fault. When I think of how I failed God and my family, it is almost impossible for me to sleep at night. What in the world am I going to do?"

I was moved to tell her, "My friend, lift up your hands, right now on this street corner, and begin to worship the Lord. Tell Him you know you are a failure, but you still love Him. Then go home and get on your knees. Don't ask God for a thing, just lift your heart and your hands and worship Him."

I left that lady standing on the street corner, with her hands raised to heaven, tears rolling down her cheeks, praising the Lord and already tasting the victory that was beginning to surge back into her life.

Now let me talk about your failure. Is there trouble in your home? Has some despised habit gripped your life so hard you can't seem to break it? Are you tormented in mind or spirit? Has God told you to do something you have failed to do? Are you out of the will of God? Are you hounded by memories of what you were at one time or by visions of what you can be? Then worship the Lord in the midst of your failure! Praise Him! Exalt Him!

All this may sound like an oversimplification, but the way past failure is simple enough for children, fools, and Ph.D.'s to follow successfully. Christ says: ". . . him that cometh to me I will in no wise cast out" (John 6:37). "Come unto me, all ye [failures] that labour and are heavy laden, and I will give you rest" (Matthew 11:28).

Don't be afraid of failure. Keep going on in spite of it. Worship God until victory comes.

The hardest part of faith is the last half hour. Keep going, and you will yet face your finest hour.

10

When You Don't Know What to Do

What would you think if our president, addressing the nation on network TV, confessed, "We really don't know what to do. Your leaders are confused, and we have no sense of direction." That would be some kind of speech. The nation would be convulsed with ridicule and scorn for him and all his associates.

That is exactly what King Jehoshaphat did. Three enemy armies were closing in on Judah, and this mighty leader called the nation together at Jerusalem to formulate a war plan. He needed plans, a decisive declaration of action. Something had to be done immediately. Instead, Jehoshaphat stood before his people and poured his heart out to God in confession:

> Behold, I say, how they reward us, to come to cast us out of thy possession, which thou hast given us to inherit. O our God, wilt thou not judge them? for we have no might against this great company that cometh against us; neither know we what to do: but our eyes are upon thee.
>
> 2 Chronicles 20:11, 12

What kind of war plan is that? No program, no committee
action. No flying banners, no bright and shiny war machinery,
no brilliant war plans. No blaring of trumpets or mustering of
patriotic armies. Just a simple confession: "We are in this over
our heads. We don't know what to do, so we will just keep our
eyes on the Lord." They decided to stand still, admit their
confusion, and put all their eggs in one basket. They would
not move anywhere but closer to their Lord; they would look
no other place for help but to Him.

Does it all sound cowardly and ridiculous? Well-armed
enemy troops surrounded them, and vultures filled the skies,
waiting for the battle to begin. They just stood together,
praising God, admitting they didn't know what to do next, and
looked only to Him for deliverance.

Nowadays when we get into trouble, we act as if we are
saying, "Lord, I love you, but I already know what I'm going
to do." When the enemy comes in like a flood, we panic. We
feel *we* must do something, make something move or give.
We have a need to see things happen, and we feel guilty if we
are not constantly proving to God how willing we are to do
anything He requires of us.

The Urge to "Make Things Happen" Comes to Us All

A divorced mother worried about her little boy's insecurity
since his dad left the home. The child wouldn't let his mother
out of his sight. He screamed and called for his daddy. All the
love this mother showered on him didn't seem to be enough.
What did this Christian mother do? She called her friends for
advice. She researched books on child raising, looking for
solutions. She went about her day in worrisome concern,
thinking to herself, "I've just got to do something about this
problem, before it gets out of hand."

There is a better way. It's absolutely scriptural for that
mother to throw up her hands and cry, "It's too much for me;

I've tried my best; I don't know whom to turn to or what to do. No one can help me, so I'll just stay close to Jesus, keep my eyes only on Him, and trust He will see me through."

A perplexed couple was on the verge of giving up. They wanted to give 100 percent to Jesus, but they had been exposed to legalistic preaching of fear, which had brought them under bondage. They got swept up into the Charismatic Movement, hoping to find joy and fulfillment. One preacher warned them, "Jesus says you must be perfect. He would never ask us to do something we couldn't do. To say you must sin a little each day is a cop-out." Another preacher said, "If you are not one hundred percent obedient, Jesus cannot save you." Another added, "Delayed obedience is disobedience. Any disobedience can damn you." Now they worry about all the things they forgot to do, about their imperfections and daily battles with the flesh, and they feel defeated.

Recently they picked up an evangelist's newsletter which warned:

> On Judgment Day there will be many Christians who have been to church three times a week, prayed in tongues, given prophecies, taught Sunday School, and served as deacons, who have not read their Bibles enough and prayed enough. God is angry with people who sin every day. He is determined to punish them eternally. There is no hope unless they stop sinning completely.

Now they also worry about not having prayed, given, and read their Bibles enough to please God. They live in constant fear. They have been told various things about their fear. Some claimed a "demon of fear" had crept into them. Others told them they were guilty of a "wrong confession," and they were urged "not to accept that fear." "Just confess victory," they were told, "and all will be well."

The wife said, "We have become so miserable in our efforts to clean ourselves up for God. Every night we evaluate our day and always feel God is displeased, because we somehow failed to behave right, confess right, or do right. We promise to do better tomorrow, but these are the things that make us want to give up and quit trying. We've lost our sense of peace and security. This is not the abundant life; it is fear. Doesn't the cross of Jesus mean more than that?"

What should they do? They wonder now who is right—the Charismatics or the Baptists. Their faith is shaken, and they have lost their sense of direction. Which teacher is right? They all seem to have such good arguments and plenty of Scriptures to prove their points. What is holiness? What does God expect? Did God do it all for me at the cross, or do I have to muster up my own strength and work out my own salvation with fear and trembling? It's very confusing!

My answer: Admit your confusion. Don't seek out pat answers to all these questions. Don't run around looking for teachers to give you solutions and answers. You don't know what to do or where to go? Good! Very good! Now you are ready to do it God's way. Now you can say with Paul, "I've decided to know nothing among you but Christ and him crucified" (*see* 1 Corinthians 2:2). Quit looking to these preachers and teachers; go yourself to the Lord. Get your eyes on Him, and, with Jehoshaphat, cry aloud: "My eyes are fixed on You!"

A couple in Iowa are trying to save their marriage. They have been married fifteen years, and the last five have been unbearable. Both have skeletons in their closets, and both have been guilty of taking their vows lightly. He cheated, and she "almost did." For five years they have tried to forgive each other, but the marriage is not fulfilling now. They pledge their love to each other, but each of them knows something is wrong. They can't put their fingers on it; they are lonely, even when together. They are not reaching each other, and the harder they try, the more frustrated they become. They'll have a good week, when everything seems to be patched up and going well; then suddenly it all breaks down, and silent anger and resentment take over. She cries herself to sleep; he thinks of giving up. In a way, they are still attracted to each other. In another way, they seem to be allergic to each other. They have tried to talk their problems through; they have made promises they couldn't keep; they have read books, seeking help; they have been to a marriage counselor. But nothing brings about an honest solution. They have both reached a place where there is no turning back. They simply do not know what to do or where to go for help.

Is there any solution? I think so. All marriages, even good ones, have their periods of stress. But some marriages can't be healed at all, outside of genuine miracles. When two people have tried everything, when it dawns on them that there is no place to go for help, when confusion and panic take over, that is when God has to intervene. Once again, all you can do in such a crisis is do as King Jehoshaphat. Don't be afraid of your confusion. You aren't the only one up against a wall. God specializes in hopeless cases. God takes over when we give up trying to work it all out ourselves. This couple with a marriage about to hit the rocks must stop looking for help outside of the Lord. They must commit their problems and their lives over to the Lord and pray, "God, it's over our heads. We've tried and failed. It looks hopeless, so we'll just stand in Your presence and look only to You for help. It's You, Lord, or nothing. Our eyes will stay fixed on You."

Reader, you too face crises in which you don't know what to do or where to go for help. What about you? Is it a financial crisis staring you right in the face? Do you live in a home situation which tears your spirit apart? Have your children hurt you, or has a child brought anguish to you? Has sickness or pain brought you down to the valley of death? Have you lost a job? Is your future scary and uncertain? Is *your* marriage in trouble? Has the death of a loved one left you depressed, lonely, and empty? Has a divorce left you feeling like a rejected failure?

Do you feel overwhelmed right now? Have you tried so many ways to see it through, yet nothing seems to help? Have you grown tired of trying? Have you almost decided there is no way out? Have you reached the end of your rope? Have you said to your heart, "I don't know what to do now!"?

We are living in a time when everything is getting shaky and insecure, and almost everybody is hurting in one way or another.

Hardly anybody knows what to do anymore. Our leaders don't have the foggiest idea of what is happening to this world or to the economy. The future is anybody's guess.

The business world is even more confused; economists are arguing with each other about what is coming. There is not a single businessman or economist in the world today who knows for certain where we are headed.

Psychologists and psychiatrists are baffled by the changing forces affecting people today. They watch the breakup of homes and marriages and become as confused as the rest of us as to why it is happening. Their reasons contradict each other.

It can even be confusing for Christians nowadays. Ministers admonish us to face our problems by looking into the Bible for ourselves, finding our own answers. But the Bible doesn't always specify "this you must do!" There is not always a direct answer for your specific problem. At times, unless the Spirit gives you a special revelation, you can get confused by verses which seem, on the surface, to be contradictory. At one place you read, "Sell all you have and give to the poor." Then you read, "If a man neglect his own house, he is worse than an infidel and has denied the faith." If you sold all and gave it away to the poor, how could you have any left to provide well for your own?

Believe it or not, even the greatest saints who ever lived did not fully understand the battle between the flesh and the spirit. Why do we have all these denominations? Why is there all the fighting over doctrine? Why are there so many disputes over baptisms, doctrines, and morals? Simply because men today are still confused and uncertain. You may think your church has all the answers, the whole truth and nothing but the truth. But it is not so! No one has it all! We are still in darkness about so many things. We all eventually reach a place, as King Jehoshaphat did. The enemy comes against us all. Some put on a big front, as though they have no fears, no questions, no problems; but they are the ones who inwardly fight the worst battles. Often those who judge everybody else and who appear so holy and righteous before others are waging a war with lust, deep inside.

Yes, we are all hurting in one way or another. We are all in need. We all reach that point of panic when the heart cries out, "What do I do now?"

Some people think I should not confess that I, too, have battles. But I do get spiritually dry at times. I do get plunged into darkness and confusion, on occasion. With Joseph, I can confess, "The Word tries me." I am no better or worse than any reader of this book. The saintliest people hurt, too. I know what King Jehoshaphat was going through. I've been there, when I had to cry aloud, "I don't know what to do, so I'll keep my eyes fixed on Him!"

You don't fold your hands, sit around at ease, and let God do it all! That is not what it means to keep your eyes fixed on the Lord. We look to the Lord, not as people who know what to do, but as people who do not know at all what they must do. We do know God is the King who sits on the flood. He is Lord of all, and we know, even if the world breaks in two, even if it all falls apart, He is a Rock of certainty. Our eyes are fixed on a risen Lord. If we do not know what to do, our faith assures us He knows what to do.

Dietrich Bonhoeffer, the German theologian, pictured the Christian as someone trying to cross a sea of floating pieces of ice. This Christian cannot rest anywhere while crossing, except in his faith that God will see him through. He cannot stand anywhere too long, or he will sink. After taking a step, he must watch out for the next step. Beneath him is the abyss, and before him is uncertainty, but always ahead of him is the Lord, firm and sure! He doesn't see the land yet, but it is there—a promise in his heart. So the Christian traveler keeps his eyes fixed upon his final place.

I prefer to think of life as more abundant and joyful than that. I picture life as a wilderness journey like that of the children of Israel. And I picture King Jehoshaphat's battle, along with all the children of Judah, as our battle. Sure, it's a wilderness. Yes, there are snakes, dry water holes, valleys of tears, enemy armies, hot sands, drought, and impassable mountains. But when the children of the Lord stood still to see His salvation, He spread a table in that wilderness and rained manna from above. He destroyed enemy armies by His power alone. He brought water out of rocks, took the poison out of snakebites, refreshed them with rain and dew, led them by pillar and cloud, gave them milk and honey, and brought them into a promised land, with a high and mighty hand. God warned them to tell every following generation: ". . . Not by might, nor by power, but by my spirit, saith the Lord of hosts" (Zechariah 4:6).

A reporter asked me to respond to a question about pressures on the church from the IRS and other government agencies. "Isn't the IRS trying to tax all evangelical ministries? Won't that day come when the government will strangle missionary and evangelical outreaches? What will you do then, seeing that these things are already in the works?"

I replied: "We are going to be forced right back into doing the work of Jesus the way He did it Himself. The day will probably come when I and all my minister friends will have to quit doing evangelism like big business and get back to New Testament methods. We will be priced out of expensive methods and go back to walking the streets with sinners, as Jesus did. As long as our eyes are focused on Jesus, no one will ever stop His message from being preached."

That Is Why Jesus Said, "I Am the Way!"

Stop searching! Stop looking in the wrong direction for help. Get alone with Jesus in a secret place; tell Him all about your confusion. Tell Him you have no other place to go. Tell Him you trust Him alone to see you through. You will be tempted to take matters into your own hands. You will want to figure things out on your own. You will wonder whether God is working at all; there will be no sign of things changing. Your faith will be tested to the limit. But nothing else works, anyway, so there is nothing to lose. Peter summed it all up: ". . . to whom shall we go? thou hast the words of eternal life" (John 6:68).

> Looking unto Jesus the author and finisher of our faith. . . .
>
> Hebrews 12:2

> Look unto me, and be ye saved, all the ends of the earth: for I am God, and there is none else.
>
> Isaiah 45:22

> . . . ye that seek the Lord: look unto the rock whence ye are hewn. . . .
>
> Isaiah 51:1

Therefore I will look unto the Lord; I will wait for the God of my salvation: my God will hear me.

Micah 7:7

He shall not be afraid of evil tidings: his heart is fixed, trusting in the Lord.

Psalms 112:7

Who is among you that feareth the Lord, that obeyeth the voice of his servant, that walketh in darkness, and hath no light? let him trust in the name of the Lord, and stay upon his God.

Isaiah 50:10

11

God Can Use You
in Spite of Your Weaknesses

God has determined to accomplish His goals, here on earth, through men with weaknesses. Isaiah, the great prayer warrior, was a man of like passions, which means he, just like the rest of us, was weak and wounded. David, the man after God's own heart, was a murdering adulterer who had no moral right to any of God's blessings. Peter denied the very Lord God of heaven, cursing the One who loved him most. Abraham, the father of nations, lived a lie, using his wife as a pawn to save his own skin. Jacob was a conniver. Paul was impatient and harsh with converts and associates who could not live up to his ascetic life-style. Adam and Eve turned a perfect marriage arrangement into a nightmare. Solomon, the wisest man on earth, did some of the most stupid things ever recorded in history. Samuel murdered King Agag in a rage of anger, in an overzealous show of righteousness. Joseph taunted his lost brothers in almost boyish glee, until the games almost backfired on him. Jonah wanted to see an entire city burn, to justify his prophecies against it; he despised the mercy of God toward a repentant people. Lot offered his two virgin daughters to a mob of sex-crazed Sodomites.

The list of men who loved God, men who were greatly used

by God, who were almost driven to the ground by their weak-nesses, goes on and on. Yet God was always there, saying, "I called you; I will be with you! I will take away the evil of your heart! I will accomplish my will, regardless!"

God's Treasure Is in Earthen Vessels

One of the most encouraging Scriptures in the Bible is 2 Corinthians 4:7: "But we have this treasure in earthen vessels, that the excellency of the power may be of God, and not of us." Then Paul goes on to describe those earthen vessels as dying men, troubled on every side, perplexed, persecuted, cast down. Even though never forsaken or in despair, those men used by God were constantly groaning under the burden of their bodies, waiting anxiously to be clothed with new ones.

God mocks man's power. He laughs at our egotistical efforts at being good. He never uses the high and mighty, but in-stead He uses the weak things of this world to confound the wise.

> For ye see your calling, brethren, how that not many wise men after the flesh, not many mighty, not many noble, are called: But God hath chosen the foolish things of the world to confound the wise; and God hath chosen the weak things of the world to confound the things which are mighty; And base things of the world, and things which are despised, hath God chosen, yea, and things which are not. . . . That no flesh should glory in his presence.
>
> 1 Corinthians 1:26–29

Wow! Does that ever describe me! Weak thing! Foolish thing! Despised thing! A base thing! A thing not very noble, not very smart, not very mighty! What insanity to think God could use such a creature! Yet that is His perfect plan and the greatest mystery on earth. God calls us in our weaknesses, even when He knows we'll do it wrong. He puts His priceless treasure in these earthen vessels of ours, because He delights in doing the impossible with nothing.

God Delights in Using Failures

God delights in using men and women who think of themselves as unable to do anything right. A woman wrote to me recently, saying:

> I'm the world's number-one failure. My marriage is failing. I seem to do everything wrong in raising my children. I'm not very good at anything. I'm not even able to understand the Bible very well. Most of it is over my head. I feel as though I'm not worth anything to anyone. I've not been a very good wife, mother, or Christian. I have to be the world's greatest failure.

She is just the kind of person the Lord is looking for: a person who knows that if anything good happens through her, it has to be God. All the hotshot Christians who go about bowling people over with their great abilities never impress God. He looked down on a scheming, base, weakling of a man called Jacob and said: "Fear not, thou worm Jacob . . . I will help thee. . . . Behold, I will make thee a new sharp threshing instrument having teeth . . . thou shalt rejoice in the Lord . . ." (Isaiah 41:14–16).

Men often use God to achieve fortune, fame, honor, and respect. Talent, personality, and cleverness are all used to advance God's kingdom, but God is not impressed. His strength is perfected in those of weakness.

When I Say Weakness, I Do Not Mean Sensuality

God does *not* use people weak in righteousness. A man's weakness can lead him into adultery, gambling, drinking, and all kinds of indulgences. God is not referring to that kind of weakness. When He calls the base, He is not referring to the wicked.

The weakness God speaks about is our human inability to obey His commandments in our own strength. God calls us to a life of holiness and separation. He tells us we can be free from the bondage of sin. His Word promises freedom from sin's power, as well as forgiveness. God's Word comes to us with some impossible challenges: "Resist the devil! Walk in the Spirit! Come out from among them! Do not commit adultery! Love your enemies! Enter into rest! Leave behind all your fears! Put down your lustful desires! Let no sin have dominion over you! As He was in this world, so be ye! Overcome self, pride, and envy! Sin not!"

Do you know how to answer that call? Think honestly about how little you can do, on your own, to fulfill these challenges; then you will realize how very weak you are. Your heart begins to cry, "Lord, how can we do such great, holy things? How are these things possible?" There is no way at all you can stand up to these commandments and challenges in your own strength and knowledge. The call to holiness is frightening and disturbing. You know what God asks of you, but you don't seem to know how to fulfill it.

Some think they can do it on their own, so they go into a convulsive concentration of all their inner resources. They grit their teeth and muster up all their human powers. They set out with great energy and resolve, calling upon all they have and taking matters into their own hands. They proceed to obey, or die trying. It works for a little while, until God crosses them up. He steps in and foils all men's schemes and self-determined efforts of the flesh. Then failure strikes, just at the moment all seemed to be going so well. These do-it-yourself Christians end up frustrated, defenseless, and weak.

That is when our Lord takes over! He comes with such a

comforting message: "Lay down your weapons. Quit trying to be so self-sufficient and strong. I am your weapon, your only weapon. I am your strength. Let Me do what you can never do. You are not supposed to do it on your own; I must do it, so you will glorify only Me. I will give you My righteousness, My holiness, My rest, and My strength. You can't save yourself; you can't help yourself; you can't please Me in any way, except by receiving the blessings of the cross, by faith. Let Me be in charge of your growth in holiness."

If You Have Too Much Going for You, God Can't Work!

Gideon is an example of a called man who had too much going for him. He was called to deliver God's children from slavery. What did he do? He blasted the trumpets and called together a mighty army. Thousands of valiant fighting men rallied under his banner, but God said to Gideon, "Your army is too great; you have too many men, too much strength. Send them back. If you win the victory with all this show of strength, you and your people might think you won on your own abilities. You have too much going for you, and I don't want you to steal the glory. Strip down your army!"

One by one, those men left Gideon's army. He must have stood by thinking, "How ridiculous! Win by weakening ourselves? God calls me to do battle, then asks me to disarm. Insanity! This is the craziest thing God has yet asked me to do. There goes my plan to become a legend in my own time."

Those fighters must have left the battlefield, shuddering with astonishment. Who ever heard of winning a battle by laying aside weapons and manpower?

From a human standpoint, it is crazy to have great victories by tiny remnants, walls tumbled without a shot fired, armies put to flight by a motley orchestra of trumpet players. By the power of faith alone, weak men confound the world.

The Way to Holiness Is Humility

No matter how powerful and honorable a man may be, God cannot use him, until he falls in the dust and gives up all his idols. Human pride must be smashed. All our boasting must be silenced. All our thoughts and plans must be abandoned. All human achievement must be recognized for what it is: filthy rags and a stench in God's nostrils.

Man must become powerless, defenseless, and hopeless in himself. He must come with fear and trembling to the cross and cry out, "Be Thou Lord of my life."

There Is Also a Weakness of the Flesh

There are Christians who fail the Lord. They love Him very much; they worry about grieving Him; but, in spite of their love and good intentions, they fall into sin. Even ministers commit adultery. Multitudes of Christians fight inner battles with lust. Their passions overrun them, and they become victims to overwhelming desires. There are modern Bathshebas and Delilahs, as well as men of God who are enticed and deceived by them.

Some of these weak children of the Lord are guilty of the sin of Peter: They have denied the Lord who called them. Others are weighed down by the guilt and condemnation of secret sins. Only God knows the battles that are fought by men and women who are among the most esteemed in the church. Those with the most acute battles often spend much of their time crying out against the sins of others, mostly to divert attention from their own struggle with the flesh.

Does God quit on any child of His who is waging a war against some white-hot passion? Does God lift His Spirit before the victory is won? Does the Lord stand nearby watching, as if to say: "You know what I expect of you. You know My laws and My commandments. When you get it right, when you wiggle free from your lust, then I'll set in motion your river of blessings. Until then, you are on your own"?

Never! Never! Instead, our Lord comes to us in our weakest moment, with sin stains blotched all over our garments, and He whispers, "My strength is for you in this your hour of weakness. Don't give up. Don't panic. Don't turn away. Don't shut Me out. Is there godly sorrow in you? Do you despise what you did? Do you want victory? Keep moving with Me. Keep moving toward Me. My arms are still stretched out, as a mother hen spreading her wings. Come, I'll protect you from the enemy."

People are giving up because they feel so weak before the power of the enemy. They say to themselves, "Why doesn't God come down and take this ugly thing out of me?"

We seem to forget God often leads us the long way around; we are seldom permitted to march straight into the Promised Land. There are lessons on faith to be learned. The wilderness temptations give God a way to show His power to deliver. Only Christians who have come through hurt, fires of temptation, and agony of defeat can really help others who hurt.

I saw Israel Narvaez, former Mau Mau gang leader, kneel and receive Christ as Lord. It was not just an emotional, surface experience; he really meant it. But Israel went back to the gang and ended up in prison as an accessory to murder. Did God quit on him? Not for one moment! Today Israel is a minister of the Gospel, having accepted the love and forgiveness of a long-suffering Saviour.

Have you failed? Is there a sin that so easily besets you? Do you feel like a weakened coward, unable to get the victory over secret sin? With that weakness in you, is there also a consuming hunger for God? Do you yearn for Him, love Him, reach to Him? That hunger and thirst is the key to your victory! That makes you different from all others who have been guilty of failing God. That sets you apart. You must keep that hunger alive. You must keep thirsting after righteousness. Never justify your weakness; never give in to it; never accept it as a part of your life.

There Is Only One Thing That Works

Faith is your victory. Abraham had weaknesses: He lied, and he almost turned his wife into an adulteress, but Abraham ". . . believed God, and it was counted unto him for righteousness" (Romans 4:3). God refused to hold his sin against him, because he believed.

Sure, you have failed—maybe yesterday, or today. Grievously! Shamefully! But do you believe Jesus has the power to ultimately free you from sin's power? Do you believe the cross of Jesus means sin's bondage is broken? Do you accept the fact that He has promised to deliver you from the snare (trap) of Satan?

Let me tell you exactly where I believe the victory is. Let your faith rise. Let your heart accept all the promises of victory in Jesus. Then let your faith tell your heart, "I may not be what I want to be yet, but God is at work in me, and He has the power to loose sin's hold on me. I'm going to keep my momentum toward the Lord, until I'm free at last. It may be little by little, but the day will come when faith will conquer. I will not always be a slave. I am not the devil's puppet. I am a weak child of God, wanting the strength of Jesus. I am not going to be another victim of the devil. I am going to come forth as pure gold, tried in the fire. God is for me. I commit it all to Him who is able to keep me from falling and present me faultless before the throne of God with exceeding great joy."

12

God Has Not Forgotten You

There is a fiery message burning in my bones. It is a message every Christian needs to hear, especially in this age of overpowering temptation and excruciating hurt.

The message I bring you from the Lord is simply this: *God has not forgotten you!* He knows exactly where you are and what you are going through right now, and He is monitoring every step along your path. But we are just as the children of Israel, who doubted God's daily care for them, even though prophets were sent to deliver wonderful promises from heaven.

God's people sat in darkness, hungry and thirsty, praying for deliverance and comfort. God bottled every tear, and He heard their cry and answered, "I will preserve you. . . . You shall no longer hunger and thirst. . . . I will have mercy on you and lead you by springs of living water . . . for the Lord will comfort his people and have mercy on all the troubled ones" (*see* Isaiah 49). Did Israel rejoice in these promises sent directly from the throne of God? Did God's people quit their fretting and begin trusting in the Lord to see them through? Did those who were hurt and confused believe a single word of these promises? "No! "But Zion said, The Lord hath forsaken me, and my Lord hath forgotten me" (Isaiah 49:14).

These were not reprobates or sons of the devil. Rather,

they were those "who sought the Lord . . . the sons of Abraham . . . those who knew righteousness . . . in whose heart
was the law of God. . . ." How much clearer must God make
His Word to these stubborn, unbelieving children? God was
greatly concerned because they were not appropriating or
hearing His promises. You can almost sense the impatience of
the Lord in rebuking their unbelief:

> I, even I, am he that comforteth you: who art thou,
> that thou shouldest be afraid of a man. . . . And forget-
> test the Lord thy maker, that hath stretched forth the
> heavens, and laid the foundations of the earth; and hast
> feared continually every day because of the fury of the
> oppressor, as if he were ready to destroy? . . ."
>
> Isaiah 51:12, 13

We Simply Ignore God's Promises

Does it all sound familiar? Here we are today, as children of
the same holy God, having in us the glorious promise of Holy
Ghost comfort; yet we go about, daily, fearing the oppressor.
We know what our Lord has promised us: guidance, peace, a
shelter from the storm, a way where there seems to be none, a
supply for every need, healing for every hurt. Do we believe
any of it? Do we just put these promises out of our minds and
go on our ways, worrying and fretting and taking matters into
our own hands? I'm afraid so! And we are all alike. We get in a
tight place; we get lonely and depressed; we fall into temptation and yield to lust; we make tragic errors and live in guilt
and terror; and through it all, we choose to forget all God has
promised us. We forget we serve a God who laid the very
foundations of this earth. We forget our Father is all-
powerful, and all things which exist were made by Him. We
see only our problems. Our fears shut out the vision of His

power and glory. We get afraid; we panic; we question; we doubt.

We forget, in our hour of need, that God has us in the palm of His hand. Instead, as the children of Israel, we are afraid we are going to blow it all and be destroyed by the enemy. How difficult it must be for our loving Father to understand why we won't trust Him when we are down and in need. God must think to Himself, "Don't they know I have graven them upon the palms of My hands? I could no more forget them in their hour of need than a mother could forget her suckling child . . . and even though a mother could forget her child, I cannot forget a single child of Mine" (*see* Isaiah 49:15, 16).

The Sin of Christians Is Unbelief

Again and again God came to Israel, pleading for their confidence and trust in times of crises. "For thus saith the Lord God, the Holy One of Israel; In returning and rest shall ye be saved; in quietness and in confidence shall be your strength: and *ye would not*" (Isaiah 30:15, *italics mine*). God said to them, "You didn't ask at My mouth or pray for help and guidance. You didn't wait for Me to help. You didn't return to Me for help and strength when you really needed it. You didn't accept My counsel; you didn't wait for Me to work. You didn't wait for that quiet word behind you that whispers, 'This is the way; walk ye in it.' You didn't believe My strong arm could deliver you. You didn't call upon My name or rest in the shadow of My palm. No! You took matters in your own hands; you depended on others; you trusted in your own thoughts. You conceived chaff and were burnt by your own fire."

God seems finally to shout at Israel:

Seek ye out of the book of the Lord, and read: no one [promise] . . . shall fail . . . for my mouth it hath com-

manded. . . . Strengthen ye the weak hands, and con-
firm the feeble knees. Say to them that are of a fearful
heart, Be strong, fear not: behold, your God will come
with vengeance, even God with a recompence; he will
come and save you. . . . Sorrow and sighing shall flee
away.

                                        Isaiah 34:16; 35:3, 4, 10

It seems to me even the New Testament echoes God's
displeasure with unbelief:

    . . . ask in faith, nothing wavering. For he that
    wavereth is like a wave of the sea driven with the wind
    and tossed. For let not that man think that he shall re-
    ceive any thing of the Lord. A double minded man is
    unstable in all his ways.

                                        James 1:6–8

Jesus was concerned that when He returned to this earth,
He would not find any faith left. He had just finished a
message about how certainly God answers prayer. He had
just promised that the heavenly Father would speedily
". . . avenge [and answer] his own elect, which cry day and
night unto him . . ." (Luke 18(7). It must have been with a
heavy heart that Jesus spoke the following: "I tell you that he
will avenge them speedily. Nevertheless when the Son of
man cometh, shall he find faith on the earth?" (Luke 18:8).

We Have Begun to Doubt That God Still Answers Prayer

Can it be that we continue in our hurt, in our sin, or in
living in defeat and failure, simply because we really do not
believe God answers our prayers anymore?

Are we as guilty as the children of Israel in thinking God
has forgotten us? Are we acting as though the Lord has forsak-

en us and given us over to our own devices, to figure things out for ourselves? Do .we really believe our Lord meant it when He said God will act just in time, in answer to our prayer of faith? Jesus implies that most of us, even though called and chosen, will not be trusting in Him when He returns. Some of God's people have already lost their confidence in Him. They do not believe, in the deepest part of their souls, that their prayers make any difference. They act as if they are all on their own.

Instead of submitting to the Lord in quiet confidence and resting in His promises, we try so hard to work out our own solutions. Then when our way of doing things blows up in our faces, we get angry with God.

A young divorcée confessed, "I almost went out to get stone drunk tonight. I've been praying for a whole year now for my husband to return, but, instead of coming back to me, he has taken up with another woman. God didn't answer my prayer, so I thought I'd go out and get drunk to show Him how angry I am." What a pity! She was ready to take it out on God because He wouldn't answer her prayer her way, on her time schedule. Like so many others who beg God for favors, she wanted only one thing: relief from her loneliness and release for her sexual drive. She didn't want more of Jesus or more holiness and Christian character. No! She simply wanted a man at her side. I knew immediately that God could not answer that woman's prayer. She was not ready to receive her husband back. She was still an emotional cripple, and she would blow it a second time. Then all she would have left would be another failure, and her despair would be compounded. God had not forsaken her; He was actually being merciful to her. He was saving her life, but she couldn't see it.

Be honest now! Has your faith been weak lately? Have you almost given up on certain things you have prayed so much about? Have you grown weary with waiting? Have you thrown up your hands in resignation, as if to say, "I just can't seem to break through. I don't know what is wrong or why my prayer is not answered. Evidently God has said no to me."

What about all the lonely people in the world who are torn apart by their solitude? What about the young, unmarried people who spend months and even years praying for a loving mate? Others would be satisfied if God would answer prayer and give them just a friend. They cry at night. The telephone becomes their lifeline, and when things get unbearable, they call someone—anyone—just to talk for a while. Does God still answer that kind of prayer? You know—the old-fashioned kind where Christian girls still pray for Christian husbands and Christian boys pray for Christian wives? Can God miraculously send friends and mates into lonely lives, in answer to prayer and faith? I still have to believe God works that way. Yet I know for a fact, after interviewing hundreds of lonely people, that few of them really believe God's promises.

Show me a lonely, hurting child of God who puts character and growth ahead of all other needs, and I'll show you one who is sure to be fulfilled. Instead of praying with faith, instead of quietly trusting His promises, instead of reading God's Word and growing in strength, instead of committing their futures to His keeping—most lonely people watch TV, read junk magazines, and grow spiritually dull. Their faith is weak because they are spiritually crippled. They pray only in quick snatches. They wallow in self-pity and self-condemnation. They are stunted and unbelieving, ready to think God has picked them out of the crowd to be treated wrongly. God can't answer their prayers, because they are not ready for friendship and true love. They would mess it up in a short time because unbelief with God always leads to instability in human relationships. I say to all lonely people: Get back to the secret closet! Get back to simple, childlike faith! Start yearning for Jesus more than for friends or mates. God will, according to His own Word, meet your every need.

God, Help Me, or I'm Going to Blow It All

Almost everywhere I go today, I hear Christians, even ministers, tell me there is something missing in their lives. A pastor friend summed it up like this: "David, I start to hunger after the Lord. I get a broken spirit; I weep and cry for hours. I feel as if something in me is seeking expression, as though a birth is about to take place. I want more from God and more out of life. I want to be holy. I want to know God and get through to Him. I pray that what I feel won't dissipate but will keep growing until I break through. But, sadly, in a few weeks, I lose my broken spirit. I go back to my old fears and dryness. I get so close, but I never go all the way. Then I say to myself, 'What happened?' "

Does that describe what you go through? Do you feel as if you are just outside the gates, so close, and about to break through to a life of joy, faith, answered prayers, and victory? Is there something in you that keeps condemning you, as if you never do enough to please God? At times do you think to yourself, "I'm just not doing anything. I'm not getting anything accomplished. I'm not growing. I'm not making real progress"?

I am of the opinion that, in all of us, just beneath the surface, there lingers a horrible thought: *Oh, God, help me, or I'm going to blow it all.* We never say it, but we think it: *God, I'm so weak, so susceptible to my besetting sin, so ignorant about winning over temptation, so confused about prayer and how to overcome the devil. I'm afraid I'll do something stupid and ruin everything.*

God Is Not a Divine Tease or Riddle

What does it all mean when prayers go unanswered, when hurts linger, when suffering is permitted to continue, and God seems to be doing nothing in response to our faith? Often God is loving us more supremely at those times than ever before. The Word says, ". . . whom the Lord loveth he chasteneth . . ." (Hebrews 12:6). A chastening of love takes precedence over every act of faith, over every prayer, over every promise. What I see as hurting in me could be His loving me. It could be His gentle hand spanking me out of my stubbornness and pride. God could be saying to me, "I've promised to meet your every need. I told you I would do anything you asked of Me in faith. You need to submit to a season of chastening; it is the only way I can make you into an experienced vessel of love. You may ask to be delivered, but it will only delay your spiritual growth. Through this suffering you will learn obedience, if you submit."

We have faith in our faith. We place more emphasis on the power of our prayers than we do on getting His power into us. We want to figure out God, so we can read Him like a book. We don't want to be surprised or bewildered. And when things happen contrary to our concept of God, we say, "That can't be God; that's not the way He works."

We are so busy working on God, we forget He is trying to work on us. That is what this life is all about: God at work on us, trying to remake us into vessels of glory. We are so busy praying to change things that we have little time to allow prayer to change us. God has not put prayer and faith in our hands as if they were two secret tools by which a select group of "experts" learn to pray something out of Him. God said He is more willing to give than we are to receive. Why are we using prayer and faith as keys or tools to unlock something that has never been locked up? It's all freely given. It's been outpoured. It's a storehouse with all the doors and windows opened, with a Father who is already at work, daily loading us with His benefits. When Jesus said, "Knock, and it shall be opened," He was talking about our doors, not His. Knock down all our own doors. We need no key to enter His presence.

Prayer is not for God's benefit; it is for ours. Faith is not for His benefit, but for ours. God is not some eternal, divine tease. He has not surrounded Himself with riddles for men to unravel, as if to say, "The wise will get the prize."

We are so mixed up on this matter of prayer and faith. We have had the audacity to think of God as our personal genie who fulfills every wish. We think of faith as a way to corner God on His promises. We think God is pleased by our efforts to back Him against the wall and shout, "Lord, You can't go back on Your promise. I want what is coming to me. You are bound by Your Word. You must do it, or Your Word is not true."

This is why we miss the true meaning of prayer and faith. We see God only as the Giver and ourselves as the receivers. But prayer and faith are the avenues by which we become the givers to God. They are to be used, not as ways to get things from God, but as ways to give Him those things by which we can please Him.

Something Better Than Answered Prayer

Do you want a promise, or do you want the Promisemaker? Do you want answers to prayer, or do you want Him who works all things together for good?

Can you imagine a wife who sticks with her husband only for the benefits she receives? She enjoys the prestige of her renowned husband, and she freely uses his name to enhance her own position. She enjoys all the luxuries he provides; she constantly spends on his credit cards. Yet she takes for granted the one who loves her so. She has little time to spend with him; she is so preoccupied with her own comfort and pleasure. How long before the world knows she uses her husband, that she is interested, not so much in him, but in what he provides?

Beloved bride of Christ, is that not the way we treat our Master? We demand the use of His credit cards, while showing so little interest in His love. All the promises are given to us so we can become partakers of Him. He wants to get His divine nature of love into our puny bodies.

Do I believe all the promises are mine? Yes! Do I believe God still answers prayer? Yes! Do I believe He will comfort me, deliver me, give me the things I need to be free and fulfilled? Yes! But all God does in me and for me depends on this one thing: I must believe He hears me when I call! He bottles every tear; He is more willing to give than I am to receive; He is most anxious to answer every prayer that will help me be more like Himself; and He will never withhold anything I need any longer than I can bear to be without it.

God has not forsaken you or me. No! A thousand times no! Right now He is wanting us all to believe He is working all things out for our good. So quit trying to figure it out! Stop worrying! Stop doubting our Lord! The answer is coming! God has not shut His ear. We will reap—in due season—if we faint not!

13

"Will God Ever Answer My Prayer?"

Have you ever asked that question? Is there one special matter you have been praying about for a long time, with no apparent answer in sight? Are there times when you wonder if the answer will ever come? Have you honestly done everything you know you should do? Have you fulfilled every requirement of prayer? Have you wept, fasted, and fervently petitioned God in true faith? And yet nothing seems to happen? If you must answer yes to all the above questions, you are in good company. You are not some strange kind of Christian, suffering chastisement from the Lord. The delayed answer to prayer is one of the most common experiences shared by even the saintliest of God's children.

I thank God for ministers and teachers who preach faith. So do I! Thank God for teachers who stir my soul to expect miracles and answers to all my prayers. Perhaps the church has become so faithless and unbelieving that God has to give us an explosive, new, and fresh revelation of His powerful promises.

There is much new teaching today on "making the right confession." Also, God's people are being urged to think positively and affirm all the promises of God. We are told to rid our lives of all hidden grudges—make all our wrongs right, even back to childhood. Lately, it has been taught that most of our unanswered prayers, our lingering illnesses, our inability to move God on our own behalf is a direct result of mishandling our faith. As one faith teacher put it, "Faith is like a faucet; you can turn it off or on."

It all sounds so simple. Do you need a financial miracle in your life? Then you are told, simply rid your life of all the hindrances, grudges, and unbelief. Confess to having already received the answer, by faith, and it will be yours. Do you want that divorced husband to return for a reconciliation? Confess it, imagine it is happening, create a mental image of a beautiful reunion, and it is all yours. Is there someone you love, who is at death's door? Then put God on notice that you will not take no for an answer; remind Him of His promises; confess healing; and it will happen, so it is taught. And if your prayer is not answered, if the husband stays away for months on end, if the sick loved one dies, if the financial need turns into a crisis, it is suggested that it is all your fault. Somewhere along the line, you allowed a negative thought to block the channel. Or you had a secret sin or unsurrendered grudge. Your confession was unscriptural or insincere. One faith teacher wrote, "If you didn't get the results I did, you aren't doing everything I did!"

I am not being facetious. I believe God answers prayer. Oh, how I do believe that! But my office is receiving tragic letters from honest Christians who are totally confused and despondent, because they can't seem to make all these new prayer-and-faith formulas work. "What's wrong with me?" writes one troubled lady. "I've searched my heart and have confessed every sin. I've bound demonic powers by the Word of God. I've fasted; I've prayed; I've confessed the promises—yet, I have not seen the answer. I must be spiritually blind, or I'm doing it all wrong."

Believe me, there are thousands of confused Christians, all across this nation, who are condemning themselves for not being able to produce an answer to a desperate prayer. They know God's Word is true, that not a single promise can fail, that God is faithful to all generations, that He is good, and that He wants His children to expect answers to their prayers. Yet, for them, there is that one prayer that goes unanswered—indefinitely. So they blame themselves. They listen to the tapes of teachers and preachers who speak so powerfully and positively about all the answers they are getting as a result of their faith. And they hear the testimonies of others who have a formula all worked out and who now receive all they ask for from God. Then they look at their own helplessness, and condemnation overwhelms them.

Let me bare my soul to you on this matter of unanswered prayers. First of all, I respect and love all the teachers and ministers of faith and positive confession. They are great men and women of God. We desperately need to be reminded of the power of faith and proper thinking. It is all very much scriptural, and those who resist or deny such teaching have probably never taken the time to hear what is truly being taught. But there is one major problem: The faith bandwagon is rolling along, full speed, on wheels that are not balanced. And if it keeps rolling in the direction it is now going, without balance, it will get sidetracked, and many trusting people will get hurt. Already some are giving up, because they have come under bondage to teachings on faith, which suggest all unanswered prayers are a result of human error. In other words, if it didn't work for you, you did something wrong; so keep doing it until you get it right.

You cannot feed your faith only on self-serving promises of healing, wealth, success, and prosperity, any more than you can grow healthy and strong eating only desserts. Faith comes by hearing "all the Word," not just preferred portions.

What about Bible truths that speak of suffering that teaches obedience? As Jesus did, we learn obedience by the things we suffer (Hebrews 5:8). There are as many Scriptures about suffering as there are about faith.

Our faith should not be afraid to investigate Bible passages that deal with God's delays, His seasons of silence, and even His sovereignty—the times when He acts without giving man an explanation.

Peter warned that faith should not stand alone. He said, ". . . add to your faith virtue; and to virtue knowledge; And to knowledge temperance; and to temperance patience . . ." (2 Peter 1:5, 6). Faith without patience and virtue and self-control (temperance) becomes self-centered and unbalanced.

All diseases are not caused by demons or evil spirits. Most are caused by a lack of self-control, gluttony, or bad habits. This belching, bloated generation stuffs itself on mountains of junk food, desserts, and poisoned beverages; then, when our bodies are weakened and stricken with disease, in panic, we run to God's Word, for a quick panacea. We will do anything to be healed—except practice self-control. And even though God, in His mercy, will often overrule our self-indulgent ways and heal our bodies, we need to invest our faith in some self-control.

There are times, in the Bible, when God could not, or did not, answer—no matter how many times it was asked for—no matter how great the faith or how positive the confession. Paul was not delivered from the affliction that buffeted him, though he prayed diligently for an answer. "For this thing I besought the Lord thrice, that it might depart from me" (2 Corinthians 12:8).

First, God wanted to see the work of grace completed in Paul. He would not permit His child to become puffed up with pride. He would not rejoice in a deliverance, but in learning how God's power could be his in times of weakness. But look what it worked out in Paul, proving God was right in not answering his request:

> . . . Most gladly therefore will I rather glory in my
> infirmities, that the power of Christ may rest upon me.
> Therefore I take pleasure in infirmities, in reproaches, in
> necessities, in persecutions, in distresses for Christ's
> sake: for when I am weak, then am I strong.
>
> 2 Corinthians 12:9, 10

Was Paul lacking in faith? full of negative thoughts? wrong
confession? Why didn't Paul preach the message we hear so
much today: "You don't have to suffer infirmities, poverty,
distresses, suffering. You don't have to put up with necessity
or weakness. Claim your victory over all suffering and
pain . . ."?

Paul wanted more than healing, more than success, more
than deliverance from prickly thorns: He wanted Christ! Paul
would rather suffer than try to overrule God. That is why he
could shout, "I glory in my present situation—God is at work
in me through all I suffer. In and through it all, I know my
present suffering cannot be compared with the glory that
awaits me."

We abuse our answers. We become ungrateful, and we so
often turn our deliverance into disaster. That's what happened to Hezekiah. God sent a prophet to warn him he was to
prepare to die, saying, "Thou shalt die, and not live."
Hezekiah wept, repented, and begged God for an additional
fifteen years. God granted his prayer. He was given a new
lease on life. The very first year into his reprieve, he com-
promised, exposing Israel to the enemy kings. He brought
disaster upon his family and his nation.

There are other times when God refuses to answer our
prayer requests, because He has a better way. He will answer, all right, but we will not recognize it as such. We will
see it as rejection, but, through it all, God will be doing His
perfect will. You find this principle at work when Israel was

being led away, captive, to the land of the Chaldeans. "What a disaster," they cried. "God has rejected our prayers; we are forsaken. God has turned a deaf ear to us." Those who were left in Jerusalem became puffed up, thinking God had heard their prayers and blessed them by permitting them to stay. But those who stayed behind were totally destroyed by sword, famine, and pestilence, until they were all consumed (Jeremiah 24:10).

But those who were taken captive were told, "You have been sent out of this place into the land of the Chaldeans for your own good . . ." (*see* Jeremiah 24:5). They never did recognize God at work, preserving a remnant, but those who were "saved through suffering" were returned to rebuild the land.

Some of My Prayers Have Not Yet Been Answered

There is an old saying, "Honest confession is good for the soul." I confess to you that I have not yet received answers to two prayers I have been praying for years. Already I hear somebody say, "Brother David, don't do that! That is negative! That is a wrong confession. No wonder you haven't received those two answers yet!" I am more amused than hurt by such comments. I refuse to ignore the facts. The facts are that I have earnestly prayed about these two matters. I have laid hold of every promise in the Bible; I have confidence that God is able to do anything; I have given my blessed Lord mountain-moving faith! Yet, the years roll by, and I have not yet seen the answers. Thousands of my prayers have been answered. I see answers to my prayers every single day of my life. God does the miraculous in my behalf, at every turn in my life. But still, those two prayers have not yet been answered.

I'll let the experts on prayer and faith try to analyze the

reasons for these unanswered prayers; but, as for me, I am not one bit worried about it. I've been all through the self-condemning bit. I've had quite enough of blaming myself for not receiving the answer when I wanted it. God is bringing a balance into my faith! My positive confession is being rechanneled in the right direction. And, oh, the joy and freedom when your faith in God no longer depends on just getting answers. What a release when your faith focuses only on Jesus and receiving His holy character.

Will My Prayers Ever Be Answered?

I believe in Holy Ghost timing. In God's own time, all our prayers will be answered, in one way or another. The trouble is, we are afraid to submit our prayers to Holy Ghost scrutiny. Some of our prayers need to be purged. Some of our faith is being misspent on requests that are not mature. We are so convinced that "if our request is in accordance to His will, we should get it." We simply do not know how to pray, "Thy will be done!" We don't want His will as much as those things permitted by His will. The only test we require of our prayers is rather self-centered: "Can I find it in God's catalog of things permitted?" So we search all through God's Word and cleverly lay out all the reasons why we should be granted certain blessings and answers. We match the promises to tailor our specific requests. When we are convinced we have a good case and have garnered enough promises, we march boldly into the presence of God, as if to say, "Lord, I've got an iron-tight case—in no way can You turn me down. I've checked my faith. I've got Your Word on the matter. I've done everything according to plan. It's mine! I claim it! Right now!"

Is that all that faith is about? simply a tool to pray out of God the benefits of promises? a challenge to His faithfulness? a test of His Word? a key to unlock God's blessing room? It seems to me we are marching into God's throne room with our faith banners waving, armed with an arsenal of promises, ready to violently claim all that is due us. All the while, we picture our approving Father congratulating us on unraveling the mystery of faith and therefore entitling ourselves to the bounties of heaven.

Until God restructures our desires and ambitions, we are going to keep on squandering our precious faith on things created, rather than the Creator. How craven and corrupt our faith becomes when it is used simply to acquire things. What a tragedy that we should boast that our faith produced for us a new car, an airplane, a financial bonanza, a new home, and so forth.

Faith is a form of thought, albeit positive, divine thought. But Jesus warned us not to give one thought to material things. "Only Gentiles [heathen] seek these things" (*see* Matthew 6:32). How very clear Jesus is on this matter, saying, "Therefore. . . . Take no thought for your life, what ye shall eat, or what ye shall drink; nor yet for your body, what ye shall put on. . . . For your heavenly Father knoweth that ye have need of all these things" (Matthew 6:25, 32).

Even the wicked prosper, at times, and it can't be said that faith produced it. God rains His love and blessings on the just, as well as the unjust. Show me a prospering Christian, and I'll show you a reprobate prospering even more.

I abhor the idea of teaching Christians how to use faith to become prosperous or more successful. That runs contrary to the teaching of the lowly Nazarene who called on His followers to sell out and give to the poor. He warned against building bigger barns and deplored the consuming hunger for worldly goods. He had no time for those who stored up treasures here on earth. He taught that His children should not become entangled with the deceitfulness of riches, but that faith should cause us to set our affection on things above.

How can it be that, with all the teaching we have today about faith, Jesus should say, ". . . Nevertheless when the Son of man cometh, shall he find faith on the earth?" (Luke 18:8). Could it be Jesus does not consider the modern brand of faith to be faith at all? Is our so-called faith so self-serving that it is becoming an abomination to the Lord? No matter how many Scriptures are quoted to support it, self-serving faith is a perversion of truth.

Compare much of the materialistic faith so prevalent today with the faith described in Hebrews 11! The things hoped for by these great men and women of God could not be measured by any worldly standard. The substance they sought was not money, houses, success, or a painless life. They exercised their faith to win God's approval of their lives. Abel's faith focused only on righteousness, and God gifted him with it. Enoch's faith was so God centered that he was translated. His faith had but one single motive: to know and please God. Faith, to Noah, meant "moving with fear" to prepare for the coming judgment. How that man would weep if he could ever witness the madness of materialism, which grips our generation.

Abraham exercised his faith to keep reminding himself he was a stranger on this earth. His blessing pact on this earth produced only a tent in which to dwell, because he put all his faith in that city whose builder and maker is God.

Some who had a reputation for having great faith ". . . received not the promise" (Hebrews 11:39). Those who did obtain promises used their faith to work righteousness, to gain strength in times of weakness, and to put the enemy to chase.

Were some of them not living in faith? Did God refuse to answer some of their prayers? After all, not all these prayer and faith warriors were delivered. Not all lived to see answers to their prayers. Not all were spared pain, suffering, and even death. Some were tortured; others were torn asunder, wandering about destitute, afflicted, tormented (*see* Hebrews 11:36–39).

These were great men and women of faith, who suffered cruel mockings, beatings, and imprisonment. They were not afflicted and tormented because of a lack of faith or a wrong confession, or because they harbored a grudge or ill will. Couldn't men of faith produce more than goatskins for their backs? Couldn't they have risen up, in faith, to claim that one great promise that no plague could come near their dwelling?

Oh, my dear friend, the world was not worthy of these saints of faith, because they had the kind of faith that crushed every claim of the flesh. Their faith had a single eye; they considered all the blessings of God as eternal and spiritual, rather than earthly and now.

Yes, I know the faith chapter closes by saying, "God has provided some better thing for us . . ." (*see* Hebrews 11:40). But how shall we define that better thing God has prepared for those who have faith today? Better health benefits? Better goatskins? Better financial arrangements? Better times of ease and prosperity? Better old-age benefits? Bigger barns, filled with all we need to retire in style?

No! I say God has provided for us something better in His only begotten Son. He came to earth as man, to show us an even greater, single-minded faith; and that is "to do the will of the Father." We should be spending more time getting into Jesus than trying to get something out of Him. We should not be praying that God make things happen *for* us, but *to* us.

Those who are so exercised in their faith for healing, for financial blessings, for solutions to problems, should, instead, focus all their faith on obtaining the "rest in Christ." There is a faith that rests not in answered prayer, but in the knowledge that our Lord will do what is right for us.

Don't worry about whether God is saying, "Yes!" or, "No!"

to your request. Don't be downcast when the answer is not in sight. Quit thinking of faith formulas and methods. Just commit every prayer to Jesus and go about your business, with confidence that He will not be one moment early or late in answering. And, if the answer you seek is not forthcoming, say to your heart, "He is all I need. If I need more, He will not withhold it. He will do it in His time, in His way; and, if He does not fulfill my request, He must have a perfect reason for not doing so. No matter what happens, I will always have faith in His faithfulness."

God help us if our faith serves the creature rather than the Creator. God forgive us if we are more concerned about getting prayers answered than in learning total submission to Christ Himself. We do not learn obedience by the things we obtain, but by the things we suffer. Are you willing to learn obedience by suffering a little longer with what appears to be unanswered prayer? Will you rest in His love, while patiently waiting for the promise, after you have done all the will of the Father?

Jettison your theology, and get back to simplicity. Faith is a gift, not a diploma. Faith should not be a burden or a puzzle. The more childlike it is, the better it works. You need no seminar or textbook; you need no guide. The Holy Spirit will lead you closer to Jesus—who is the Word—by whom cometh faith.

14

Jesus and Storms

Jesus ordered His disciples into a boat that was headed for a collision. The Bible says He constrained them to get into a ship. It was headed for troubled waters; it would be tossed about like a bobbing cork. The disciples would be thrust into a mini-Titanic experience, and Jesus knew it all the time. "And straightway Jesus constrained his disciples to get into a ship, and to go before him unto the other side, while he sent the multitudes away" (Matthew 14:22).

Where was Jesus? He was up in the mountains overlooking that sea; He was there, praying for them not to fail in the test He knew they must go through. The boat trip, the storm, the tossing waves, and the winds were all a part of a trial the Father had planned. They were about to learn the greatest lesson they would ever learn. That lesson was how to recognize Jesus in the storm.

They recognized Him to this point as the Miracle Worker, the Man who turned loaves and fishes into miracle food, the Friend of sinners, the One who brought salvation to every kind of lost humanity. They knew Him as the Supplier of all their needs, even to paying their taxes from a fish's mouth.

They recognized Jesus as the Christ, the very Son of God. They knew He had the words of eternal life. They knew He had power over all the works of the devil. They knew Him as a teacher, having taught them how to pray and forgive, to bind and loose.

But they had never learned to recognize Jesus in the storm. Tragically, those disciples who thought they really knew Him best could not recognize Him when the storm hit.

That's the root of most of our trouble today. We trust Jesus for miracles and healing. We believe Him for our salvation and the forgiveness of our sins. We look to Him as the supplier of all our needs. We trust Him to bring us into glory one day. But, when a sudden storm falls upon us, and it seems as if everything is falling apart, we find it difficult to see Jesus anywhere near. We can't believe He allows storms to teach us how to trust. We are never quite sure He is nearby when things really get rough.

The ship is now tossing; it appears to be sinking; winds are blowing; they have everything going contrary to them.

> But the ship was now in the midst of the sea, tossed with waves: for the wind was contrary. And in the fourth watch of the night Jesus went unto them, walking on the sea. And when the disciples saw him walking on the sea, they were troubled, saying, It is a spirit; and they cried out for fear. But straightway Jesus spake unto them, saying, Be of good cheer; it is I; be not afraid.
>
> Matthew 14:24–27

They were so suddenly swamped, so suddenly overwhelmed; the very thought that Jesus was nearby, watching over them, was absurd. One probably said, "This is the work of Satan; the devil is out to kill us because of all those miracles we've had a part in."

Another probably said, "Where did we go wrong? Which one of us has sin in his life? Let's have a heart searching; let's confess one to another. God is mad at somebody on this boat!"

Another could have said, "Why us? We're doing what He said to do. We're obedient. We're not out of God's will. Why all of a sudden this storm? Why would God allow us to be shaken up so much, on a divine mission?"

In their dárkest hour, Jesus went to them. How difficult it must have been for Jesus to wait on the edge of that storm, loving them so much, feeling every pain they felt, wanting so much to keep them from getting hurt, yearning after them as a father for his children in trouble. Yet, He knew they could never fully know Him or trust Him, until the full fury of the storm was upon them. He would reveal Himself only when they had reached the limit of their faith. The boat would never have gone down, but their fear would have drowned them more quickly than the waves beating on the ship. The only fear of drowning was that of drowning from despair, fear, and anxiety—not water.

Remember, Jesus can calm that sea at any time, simply by speaking the word, but the disciples cannot. Could faith on their part have been exercised? Could not they command the sea in Jesus' name? ("Greater works shall ye do.") Could not the promises have been put into practice? ("All things asked in prayer . . . ye shall have!") These cannot happen until we have learned to recognize Jesus in the storm, have received faith to ride out the storm, and have learned to be of good cheer when the boat appears to be sinking.

When the disciples saw Jesus, they thought it was a spirit, a ghost. They did not recognize Jesus in that storm. They saw a ghost, an apparition. The thought of Jesus being so near, so much a part of what they were going through, did not even enter their minds.

The Greatest Danger

Here is the danger we all face: not being able to see Jesus in our troubles—instead we see ghosts. In that peak moment of fear when the night is the blackest, the storm is the angriest, the winds are the loudest, and the hopelessness the most overwhelming, Jesus always draws near to us, to reveal Himself as the Lord of the flood, the Saviour in storms. "The Lord sitteth upon the flood; yea, the Lord sitteth King for ever" (Psalms 29:10).

The disciples compounded their fears. Now, not only were they afraid of the storm, they had a new fear: ghosts. The storm was spewing up ghosts; mysterious spirits were on the loose.

You would think at least one disciple would have recognized what was happening and said, "Look friends, Jesus said He would never leave us or forsake us. He sent us on this mission; we are in the center of His will. He said the steps of a righteous man are ordered by Himself. Look again. That's our Lord! He's right here! He's never been far away. We've never once been out of His sight. Everything's under control."

But not one disciple could recognize Him. They did not expect Him to be in their storm. They expected Him at the Samaritan well. They expected Him to be there with outstretched arms, bidding little children to come. They expected Him to be in the temple, driving out the money changers. And they expected Him to one day be at the right hand of the Father, to make them kings and priests. But never, never did they expect Him to be with them, or even near them, in a storm!

It was, to them, just an act of destiny; an unexpected disaster; a tragic accident of fate; an unwanted, unexpected, unnecessary trial; a lonely, fearful journey into darkness and despair. It was a night to be forgotten!

God saw that storm through different eyes. It was as much a test for these disciples as the wilderness was for Jesus. God took them away from the miracles, shut them up in a tiny, frail boat, far from the upper room, then turned nature loose. God allowed them to be shaken but not sunken.

The Greatest Lesson

There was only one lesson to be learned, only one. It was a simple lesson, not some deep, mystical, earth-shattering one. Jesus simply wanted to be trusted as their Lord, in every storm of life. He simply wanted them to maintain their cheer and confidence, even in the blackest hours of trial. That's all.

Jesus did not want them to conjure up ghosts; but they did, just as we all still do. Jesus must have appeared as twelve different ghosts in the twelve separate minds of those disciples.

Perhaps one thought to himself, "I know that ghost: that's the ghost of lying. I lied a few weeks back. That's what this storm is all about. That's the reason we're in trouble: I lied. That's the ghost of lying trying to warn me to quit lying. I will! I will! Just get me out of this mess, and I'll quit lying."

Another probably thought, "That's the ghost of hypocrisy! I'm two-faced. I'm a phony. Now I can see what I am in this storm. That's why the storm. God sent that ghost to warn me to straighten up. I will! I will! I will! No more hypocrisy! Just please deliver me!"

Another: "That's the ghost of compromise. I've been compromising lately. Oh, my. I've really failed the Lord. It's been a secret thing I tried to hide, but I'm scared now. You allowed this storm; You sent that ghost to warn me to get back to holiness. I will! I will! Just give me another chance."

Another: "That's the ghost of covetousness. I've been too materialistic."

Another: "That's the ghost of wasted time. I've grown lazy. I've not been witnessing. I've grown cold, lukewarm, but now I've learned my lesson!"

Another: "That's the ghost of grudges. I've not been forgiving as I should. I've been avoiding certain people. That's why God is shaking me up, to teach me to quit holding grudges."

Another: "That's the ghost of secret sin; evil thoughts. I

can't seem to give them up, so God had to send this storm to expose me."

Another: "That's the ghost of broken promises. I promised God I'd do this thing, and I didn't do it. Now God is getting back at me. He's mad at me, so He put me out in this storm. I'm sorry. That's the lesson; I've learned my lesson!"

No! No! A thousand times no! Those are all ghosts of our own minds, apparitions only. None of these are the real lessons to be learned. God is not mad at you. You are not in a storm because you failed. These ghosts are not even in your storm.

It is Jesus at work, seeking to reveal Himself in His saving, keeping, preserving power! He is wanting you to know the storm has one purpose only—and that is to bring you to complete rest and trust in His power and presence at all times, in the middle of miracles and in the middle of storms. It is so easy, in a storm, to lose a sense of His presence and feel we are left alone, to battle against hopeless odds; or that somewhere along the line, as a result of sin or compromise, Christ has forsaken us and left us out there, all alone, in that tossing boat.

What about those times when the contrary winds are sickness, disease, and pain? What about when cancer strikes? What about when pain and fear are so overwhelming, you can't spare a thought about the closeness of Jesus? Your sudden storm is upon you, and there is no other thought that survival. You don't want to die; you want to live. You see the ghost of death in the shadows, and you tremble. You don't have the strength to face even the next hour.

That is what the presence of Jesus is all about. It is a revelation that is the most powerful when it comes to us at that most-needed time.

15

The Ultimate Healing

Resurrection from the dead is the "ultimate healing." I tried to share that glorious truth with the grieving parents of a five-year-old boy who had died, just hours before, of leukemia. They had begged God for the healing of their dear child. The whole church prayed earnestly. Friends had prophesied: "He will not die; he will be healed." One week prior to the little boy's death, the heartbroken father picked up the fevered child and walked him around the room. "God, I'll not give him up. Your promises are true. My faith has never faltered. More than two or three have agreed in Your name that he should be healed. I confess it now, and I claim it." In spite of everything, the child died.

I was there when that child was laid out in a tiny casket. I looked, with horror, on all those sad faces of Christian friends who had gathered to mourn his death. The parents were in a state of shock. Everybody was afraid to speak out what they were thinking. I know the church people were thinking it, and the pastor acted as if he was thinking it. I know the parents were certainly thinking it. And just what was this unthinkable thought gripping their minds? Simply this: *God did not answer prayer! Someone goofed! Someone stood in the way of God's healing power! Someone is responsible for this child's death, because of a grudge, a hidden motive, or a secret sin. Someone or something hindered the healing.*

It was there and then that a glorious truth dawned on me, and I took the parents aside and briefly unburdened my heart, "Don't question God," I said. "Your prayers have all been answered. God gave your son the ultimate healing. That little, fevered, diseased body has been abandoned; and Ricky is right now clothed in his perfect, painless body. Ricky has been healed! God did exceedingly above all you could ask or think of Him. He is alive and well—all that has changed is his body and his location!"

Those parents turned on me with anger. They were bitter and confused, and they left the graveside to enter a bleak five-year period of doubts, questions, guilt, and self-examination. During that time, they would hardly speak to me. But God, in His mercy, always breaks through to sincere hearts. One day, while in prayer, the Holy Spirit came upon that grieving mother, reminding her of my message. She began praising the Lord, saying, "Ricky was healed. God did answer our prayers. Lord, forgive our doubts. Ricky is right now alive and well and enjoying his healing."

I treasure the moment we stood together, arms entwined, thanking the Lord for such comfort. Ricky's father confessed, "Dave, we were so angry with you. We thought you were heartless, suggesting our son, who had just died, had been healed. Now we understand. We were so selfish; we could not understand what was best for our son. We thought only of our own pain, our grief, our suffering. But now the Lord has shown us that Ricky was not destroyed by death, but the Lord drew him to Himself."

The Life Is Not in the Shell

These mortal bodies of ours are but mere shells, and the life is not in the shell. The shell is not for keeping, but a temporary confine that enshrouds an ever-growing, ever-maturing life force. The body is a shell that acts as a transient guardian of the life inside. The shell is synthetic in comparison to the eternal life it clothes.

Every true Christian has been imbued with eternal life. It is planted as a constantly maturing seed in our mortal bodies. It is, within us, an ever-growing, ever-expanding process of development; and it must eventually break out of the shell, to become a new form of life. This glorious life of God in us exerts pressure on the shell, and, at the very moment resurrection life is mature, the shell breaks. The artificial bonds are broken, and, like a newborn baby chick, the soul is freed from its prison. Praise the Lord!

Death is but a mere breaking of the fragile shell. At the precise moment our Lord decides our shell has served its purpose, a sudden rush of eternal life floods the soul, and God opens the shell—only to free the new creature that has come of age.

As life itself abandons the shell, after it has fulfilled its function, so must God's people abandon their old, corrupt bodies made from the dust from which they came. Who would think of picking up the fragmented pieces of shell and forcing the newborn chick back into its original state? And who would think of asking a departed loved one to give up his new, glorified body—made in Christ's own image—and return to the decaying shell from which he broke free?

To Die Is Gain?

Paul said it: "To die is gain"! (Philippians 1:21). That kind of talk is absolutely foreign to our modern spiritual vocabularies. We have become such life worshipers, that we have very little desire to depart to be with the Lord.

Paul said, "For I am in a strait betwixt two, having a desire to depart, and to be with Christ; which is far better" (Philippians 1:23). Yet, for the sake of edifying the converts, he thought it best to "stay in the shell." Or, as he put it, "live in the flesh" (v. 22).

Was Paul morbid? Did he have an unhealthy fixation with death? Did Paul show a lack of respect for the life God had blessed him with? Absolutely not! Paul lived life to the fullest. To him, life was a gift, and he had used it well to fight a good fight. He had overcome the fear of the "sting of death" and could now say, "It's better to die and be with the Lord than to stay in the flesh."

Those who die in the Lord are the winners; we who remain are the losers. How tragic that God's people still look upon the departed as losers—poor, miserable souls, cheated out of a greater measure of life. Oh! But if our spiritual eyes and ears could be opened but for a few moments, we would see our dear, loved ones on God's side of the universe, walking in the pure, crystal river of eternal life, trying to shout at us, "I won! I won! I'm free at last! Press on, dear earthlings; there is nothing to fear. Death does not sting. It is true: It is better to depart and to be with the Lord."

Did someone you love break out of his shell? Were you there when it happened? Or did the news reach you by phone or telegram? What kind of horrifying feeling rushed through your mind when 'you were told, "He is dead!" or "She is dead!"?

Certainly it is natural to mourn and weep for those who die. Even the death of the righteous is painful for those left behind. But, as followers of the Christ who holds the keys of death in His hand, we dare not think of death as an accident perpetuated by the devil. Satan cannot destroy a single child of God. Satan, though permitted to touch Job's flesh and afflict his body, could not take his life. God's children always die right on His schedule, not one second too soon or too late. If the steps of a righteous person are ordered by the Lord, He orders the final one, too.

Death is not the ultimate healing: Resurrection is! Death is the passage, and sometimes that passage can be painful, even excruciating. I have seen many of God's chosen people die in tremendous pain. But Paul answers that well by proclaiming "For I reckon that the sufferings of this present time are not worthy to be compared with the glory which shall be revealed in us" (Romans 8:18). No matter how much pain and suffering wreak havoc on these bodies, it is not even worthy to be compared with the unspeakable glory that awaits those who endure the passage.

God's Magnetic Pull

In my years of watching the body die, I have noted one common experience. I call it "the magnetic pull." I'm convinced that death comes to the saint long before the last breath is taken. When the Lord turns the key, an irreversible magnetic pull of God's Spirit begins to draw the loved one to Himself. Somehow, God permits that person who is being drawn to know it is happening. He is given an inner knowledge that he is going home. He has already seen a bit of the heavenly glory. While loved ones gather around him to plead for his resurrection, you can sense he doesn't want to stay imprisoned in his shell any longer. A crack has appeared; he has peered through and has glimpsed the New Jerusalem, with all its exciting eternal joys. He has seen a vision of the glories awaiting him. To turn back would be emptiness.

Recently, I stood by the bedside of a saintly mother who was dying of cancer. Her hospital room was aglow with God's holy presence. Her husband and children were softly singing hymns; and, as weak as she was, she lifted her face heavenward and whispered, "I feel His pull. It's true, He does draw us to Himself. It feels like a powerful magnet, and I'm going faster and faster, and I don't want anybody to stop me, now." Within hours, she broke through her fleshy shell, into God's inner circle. In that holy hour, no one dared interfere with this divine process of changing, when the terrestrial was being swallowed up by the celestial.

It's so sad to hear Christians condemn God for taking their loved ones from them. "Lord, it's just not fair," they argue. Though it is difficult to condemn what people say in times of deep grief, I believe such questioning can be selfish. We think only of our loss, and not their gain. God only plucks out of this world those He can no longer love at a distance. The mutual love of God and the believer demands that he be in His presence. It is then love is perfected. To be with the Lord is to experience His love in its fullness.

So you stand helplessly by, as your loved one enters that passage called death. You know it's a dark, lonely path, and you can hold that hand only so far. The time comes when you have to let that loved one go and let Jesus take him by the hand. He is no longer yours; he belongs to Him. You feel so helpless, but there is not one thing you can do, but rest in the knowledge that the Lord has taken over and that your loved one is in good hands. Then, in a moment, he is out of sight. The battle is over. Only the broken shell remains. The delivered soul has taken flight into God's holy presence. The death of the righteous is a precious thing. David, the Psalmist, wrote, "Precious in the sight of the Lord is the death of his saints" (Psalms 116:15). God looks upon the death of one of His children as a cherished moment. But we humans find little or nothing to cherish in this experience.

A young mother told me a pitiful story of the trauma she endured after the death of her two children. The first child died at the age of eighteen months. The second lived only about two months. She had thought God had given her the second child to make up for the loss of the first—now both were dead. She and her Christian husband went through months of self-examination. Was there sin in their lives? Had they angered God by doubting His healing power? Were they in some way responsible for the deaths of their children? Then, one dark day, a "good Christian friend" came to them with what she declared to be a message from the Lord. They were, she said, being chastised by the Lord for hidden grudges and dishonesty in their marriage. "Those children would still be alive," they were told, "if your hearts had been purged of sin and if your confession had been right."

They were crushed to despair. But God, in His mercy, showed them how ridiculous such thoughts were. Such teaching is tragic nonsense. God doesn't play Russian roulette with lives!

Shall we quit praying for the dying? Shall we give up on the terminally ill? Should we just lie down and die, if that is ultimate healing? Never! More than ever in my life, I believe in divine healing. We should pray for everybody to be healed. And the only people who are not healed, according to our concept of healing, are those who are chosen for His ultimate healing. Some are not given restored organs or limbs; instead, they are given the perfect healing: glorified, painless, eternal bodies. What is there that our minds can conceive as being a greater miracle than resurrection from the dead?

We Are Too Earthbound

Any message about death bothers us. We try to ignore even thinking about it. We suspect those who talk about it of being morbid. Occasionally we will talk about what heaven must be like, but, most of the time, the subject of death is taboo.

How different the first Christians were! Paul spoke much about death. In fact, our resurrection from the dead is referred to in the New Testament as our "blessed hope." But, nowadays death is considered an intruder that cuts us off from the good life we have been accustomed to. We have so cluttered our lives with material things; we are bogged down with life. The world has trapped us with materialism. We can no longer bear the thought of leaving our beautiful homes, our lovely things, our charming sweethearts. We seem to be thinking, "To die now would be too great a loss. I love the Lord, but I need time to enjoy my real estate. I'm married. I've yet to prove my oxen. I need more time."

Have you noticed there is very little talk, nowadays, about heaven or about leaving this old world behind? Instead, we are bombarded with messages on how to use our faith to acquire more things. "The next revival," said one such well-known teacher, "will be a financial revival. God is going to pour out financial blessings on all believers."

What a stunted concept of God's eternal purposes! No wonder so many Christians are frightened by the thought of death. The truth is, we are far from understanding Christ's call to forsake the world and all its entanglements. He calls us to come and die, to die without building memorials to ourselves, to die without worrying how we should be remembered. Jesus left no autobiography, no headquarters complex, no university or Bible college. He left nothing to perpetuate His memory but the bread and the wine.

What is the greatest revelation of faith, and how is it to be exercised? You will find it in Hebrews:

> These all died in faith . . . confessing that they were strangers and pilgrims on the earth. . . . But now they desire a better country, that is, an heavenly: wherefore God is not ashamed to be called their God: for he hath prepared for them a city.
>
> *See* Hebrews 11:13, 16

Here is my honest prayer to God:

Lord, help me cut loose from the bondage of things. Let me not squander my gift of life on my own selfish pleasures and goals. Help me to bring all my appetites under Your control. Make me remember I am a pilgrim, not a settler. I am not Your fan, but Your follower. Most of all, deliver me from the bondage of the fear of death. Make me finally understand that to die in Christ is gain. Help me to look forward, with precious anticipation, to my moment of ultimate healing.

I am he that liveth, and was dead; and, behold, I am alive for evermore. . . .

Revelation 1:18

. . . through death he might destroy him that had the power of death, that is, the devil; And deliver them who through fear of death were all their lifetime subject to bondage.

Hebrews 2:14, 15

But is now made manifest by the appearing of our Saviour Jesus Christ, who hath abolished death, and hath brought life and immortality to light through the gospel.

2 Timothy 1:10